"I welcome any book that seeks to eq[...] [...]ong in their walk with God—regardless [...] [...]eld—and effective in their work and in their te[...] [...] missions effort needs this type of input and help."

Andrew Scott, president, Operation Mobilization, USA

"I am thrilled with the insights and practical truth Ryan Shaw has brought together here. According to Hudson Taylor, the real secret for modern-day message bearers is a life and vibrant inner core of ever-developing faith and intimacy with God. The keys identified here are right on to unlock the potential Jesus promised!"

Donnie Scearce, lead pastor, North Park Church, London, Ontario, Canada

"Ryan provides ten fundamental spiritual keys that will equip you to yield fruit-bearing results and ensure this mandate is achieved. Yet, by cultivating these keys or inner-life qualities, a whole new understanding will take hold that it is not ultimately about accomplishing an assignment but pleasing the heart of God."

Ché Ahn, senior pastor, HRock Church, Pasadena, California; president, Harvest International Ministry

"Finally! For years the mission engine of our world has lacked a book like this. Spiritual formation and discipleship are at the core of effective and fruitful mission. . . . Ryan's book couldn't come at a more timely moment for the mission world. I pray that this book gets into the hands of as many mission workers as possible. It's that important, and it's that good!"

Joseph W. Handley Jr., president, Asian Access

"Message bearers are people wholeheartedly committed to serving Jesus and inviting others to come with them on the journey. Ryan unpacks the importance of being a serious message bearer and the means we can use of setting our hearts toward consistent growth so that we become more effective."

Bob Creson, president/CEO, Wycliffe Bible Translators, USA

"This is an important book about the most fundamental principles in mission that gives us a deeper understanding of what it means to be a message bearer. Beyond a doubt it is an inspiring and tremendous help for those who want to invest their lives for the extension of the kingdom of God. Ryan Shaw is a gifted writer with profound insights who makes the biblical text come alive."

Martha Roguin de Rodriguez, president of COMIBAM Argentina

"This excellent book is indispensable to all who are called to serve the Lord in advancing his kingdom, but also to those who train and send missionary workers. It helps us to understand the crucial importance of a healthy spiritual formation in the effort to fulfill the demands of the Great Commission."

Bertil Ekstrom, executive director, World Evangelical Alliance Mission Commission

"This book brings focus to some of the most fundamental topics as we consider how we have done in our Great Commission work so far and is definitely an excellent tool for how to do it well in the coming years."

Decio de Carvalho, executive director, COMIBAM International

"Ryan Shaw writes about the basics of Christian spiritual disciplines for those who want to obey our Lord's Great Commission seriously—to make history and effect transformation among the nations. . . . This book will be an excellent guide for all who seek to fulfill God's will in our generation."

David S. Lim, national director, Philippine Missions Association

"Ryan's book offers powerful spiritual keys to every message bearer. I keep thinking how desperately the emerging mission movement needs to hear such messages that point to the necessity of being spiritually grounded as the primary and vital resource for success in any mission enterprise."

Daniel Bourdanné, general secretary, International Fellowship of Evangelical Students

"Most of us focus on strategy, methods and materials, but Ryan helps us look beyond just purpose and plans, and evaluate the person. . . . *Spiritual Equipping for Mission* is a challenge for any world changer who wants to know and live and share the heart of God with those who desperately need to experience the love of the Savior."

Steve Shadrach, executive director, Center for Mission Mobilization

"The spiritual keys that Ryan puts forth are indispensable to the formation of the heart and life of any message bearer and will fuel the fire of even the most experienced person already engaged in kingdom work. I highly recommend this book as a training resource, as an instrument for personal challenge and inspiration, and as a handbook for being a disciple-making message bearer."

John Brown, senior pastor, Harmony Vineyard Church, Kansas City, Missouri

"Ryan Shaw has presented ten issues that are key for anyone wanting to be serious about crosscultural message bearing. While much crosscultural training is focused on strategy and methodology, Ryan deals with core issues of who the message bearer is to be and how they can remain alive in their inner being."

Betty Sue Brewster, Fuller Theological Seminary, School of Intercultural Studies

"Ryan Shaw has clearly identified a gap in the area of motivating and training crosscultural Christian workers in this generation. By paying attention to the prevailing omission of focus on spiritual dimensions in the missionary enterprise, he proceeds to invite the church back to the foundations of a God-filled life as the primary qualification for effective ministry engagement."

Thuo Mburu, consultant, Trinity Fellowship, Nairobi, Kenya

SPIRITUAL EQUIPPING FOR MISSION

THRIVING AS GOD'S MESSAGE BEARERS

RYAN SHAW

FOREWORD BY TOM LIN

IVP Books

An imprint of InterVarsity Press
Downers Grove, Illinois

InterVarsity Press
P.O. Box 1400, Downers Grove, IL 60515-1426
World Wide Web: www.ivpress.com
Email: email@ivpress.com

©2014 by Ryan Shaw

All rights reserved. No part of this book may be reproduced in any form without written permission from InterVarsity Press.

InterVarsity Press® is the book-publishing division of InterVarsity Christian Fellowship/USA®, a movement of students and faculty active on campus at hundreds of universities, colleges and schools of nursing in the United States of America, and a member movement of the International Fellowship of Evangelical Students. For information about local and regional activities, write Public Relations Dept., InterVarsity Christian Fellowship/USA, 6400 Schroeder Rd., P.O. Box 7895, Madison, WI 53707-7895, or visit the IVCF website at www.intervarsity.org.

All Scripture quotations, unless otherwise indicated, are taken from The Holy Bible, New King James Version, NKJV. *Copyright © 1982 by Thomas Nelson, Inc.*

While all stories in this book are true, some names and identifying information in this book have been changed to protect the privacy of the individuals involved.

Cover design: Cindy Kiple
Interior design: Beth Hagenberg
Images: Christo Nicolle/Getty Images

ISBN 978-0-8308-3672-7 (print)
ISBN 978-0-8308-9658-5 (digital)

Printed in the United States of America ♾

 As a member of the Green Press Initiative, InterVarsity Press is committed to protecting the environment and to the responsible use of natural resources. To learn more, visit greenpressinitiative.org.

Library of Congress Cataloging-in-Publication Data

Shaw, Ryan.
  Spiritual equipping for mission : thriving as God's message bearers / Ryan Shaw.
    pages cm
  Includes bibliographical references.
  ISBN 978-0-8308-3672-7 (pbk. : alk. paper)
  1. Missionaries—Religious life. I. Title.
  BV2063.S487 2014
  266—dc23

                                                      2014022817

P 23 22 21 20 19 18 17 16 15 14 13 12 11 10 9 8 7 6 5 4 3 2

Y 33 32 31 30 29 28 27 26 25 24 23 22 21 20 19 18 17 16 15

To Dan and Georgia Shaw

and Alex and Mary Fife

Much of the teaching in this book has been gleaned

through learning from you. You have taught us to

spiritually thrive in serving God. In a day when solid

examples of godly parents are few, you have shined

brightly as stars for Kelly and me. You are parents,

in-laws, but more than this, you are our

closest friends and mentors.

Thank you.

Contents

Foreword

As a leader of several large missions organizations and movements, I'm passionate about God's global mission and am always looking for new opportunities as well as new ways to work more effectively and efficiently. For years, I leaned heavily toward planting ministries where none existed, moving five times to different countries and states in the span of ten years, and running at an incredible pace. But as much as I was caring about the souls of many others around the world, I began to find that it was challenging to care for *my own* soul.

One of my moves was to Mongolia, a country that only recently opened to the gospel, with the first complete Bible translated in the year 2000. One of the most breathtaking sights in Mongolia is the Gobi Desert, which spans over a thousand miles from west to east and six hundred from north to south. It's extremely dry and barren: rainfall in most parts is less than four inches per year. Virtually no people, no vegetation and no livestock can survive in the Gobi. Though I was unable to visit it, my family and I certainly had our share of *desert experiences* while serving as missionaries.

The mission field was spiritually isolating. There were no churches that we felt at home in, and the church we decided on didn't speak any English. Listening to the worship songs and sermons with our limited language abilities and limited cultural understanding made church a place where we experienced stress rather than the presence of God. There was no high-speed Internet to get sermons online, no access to Christian retreat centers. Reading my handful of English-language InterVarsity Press books during winter's subzero temperatures and frequent electrical outages nurtured my soul only for a few minutes at a time. There were no spiritual companions or friends in our city, which made it difficult for us to replicate the tight-knit small-group community that had kept us spiritually accountable in America. My wife and I often looked at each other sadly and confessed, "We have no friends."

It was difficult going through these desert experiences. From the outside, the ministry looked fruitful and even glamorous at times, but our inner lives were withering and ugly.

Of course, desert experiences aren't just limited to Mongolia. All of us who strive to accomplish the Great Commission go through dry seasons. You may have picked up this book because you're in one of those seasons. Most of us want something more for our spiritual lives, or perhaps we hope to cultivate practices that will sustain us through future desert seasons.

In this book, my friend Ryan Shaw does an outstanding job of equipping current and future Great Commission workers for all kinds of desert seasons and difficult mission fields. He identifies one of the most urgent and strategic issues in the mission field today: *nurturing the spiritual life of the missionary.*

In our passionate pursuit of God's global mission, church and mission leaders around the world have in recent decades practiced what Dallas Willard called a "great omission" from the Great Commission. We have omitted the making of disciples and neglected to enroll Christ's workers as Christ's students. As a result, the non-disciple "has something 'more important' to do or undertake than to become like Jesus Christ."[1] We see nondisciples working feverishly at important missionary tasks such as culture learning, preparing sermons or publicly proclaiming the gospel. But there is a hidden cost of nondiscipleship: losing out on everlasting peace and love, power from the Holy Spirit and perseverance that helps us survive life's desert seasons. It's important to remember this cost when discipleship is difficult.

I know Ryan to be a sacrificial servant, willing to give his life to see unengaged people groups come to know Christ. He rightfully challenges us not to fall into the temptation of emphasizing the mission at the expense of our own souls. Ryan also brings this pastoral vision down to a practical level, giving us very helpful "spiritual keys" that will help us cultivate a deeper spiritual life. If we heed his words and apply these keys, I believe we will not only be more spiritually equipped, but also will spiritually *thrive* in engaging the Great Commission. May it be so!

Tom Lin
Vice President of Missions, InterVarsity Christian Fellowship/USA
Director, Urbana Student Missions Conference
Author, Pursuing God's Call

Introduction

Setting the Stage

Over the past few decades, considerable global momentum has been building related to the Great Commission. Networks, strategies, partnerships and niche ministries have been raised up to focus on specific needs. More believers around the world are being activated in crosscultural ministry than ever before. We praise the Lord for these exciting trends. However, for them to reach their potential, a deeper level of spirituality is needed.

Christian individuals, leaders, ministries and organizations have at times been guilty of resorting to techniques and forms instead of spiritual reality. It isn't uncommon to attend a mission conference or listen to a mission speaker and hear little about the depth of spiritual quality necessary to produce fruitfulness among the nations. Mostly, we hear of the needs of the world and of strategies for reaching people.

This is nothing new. Yet the current prevalence is a cause for concern. The often-shallow state of the global church's spiritual life results in an inability to overcome challenges, a misinterpretation of events and a tendency to inadvertently malign the testimony of

Christ. Most people have good intentions in serving God, but over time those intentions prove inadequate. Is it good enough to have the latest strategy or technique? Or do we need more to fuel and sustain the work of crosscultural mission?

As a message bearer, I've seen the effects of the neglect of spiritual equipping. I've traveled in more than fifty nations, and over the past eleven years, my family has lived in Canada, Turkey and Thailand. I've marveled at how some message bearers deliberately develop their spiritual lives, and I've seen the accompanying fruit. But I've also been heartbroken by countless stories of great potential cut short by spiritual neglect. I've watched promising disciples who seemed perfectly fit for mission become crosscultural message bearers. Yet, after a few years, they were back in their home country, burned out, defeated and disillusioned with God and his work in the world. This often left a stain among the people they worked with. What happened? Many overlooked the development of the ten spiritual keys discussed in this book.

All of us want to know what's necessary for the power of God to work through us. What's required for the presence of God to make an eternal impact among those we serve? Nobody gets involved in crosscultural ministry to fail. Yet we're rarely taught ways to thrive spiritually; it seems the assumption is that we intuitively know how.

The Great Commission is a spiritual work, not merely a strategic one. It's effectively served through spiritual people, full of the Holy Spirit, obedient to Jesus, consistently tending the garden of their inner life.

JESUS' GREAT COMMISSION

Jesus' final words, given forty days after his resurrection and before he ascended to the right hand of the Father, have become known as his Great Commission. Final words carry considerable weight. This is why we value the last will and testament of a person. Multitudes of Scriptures (Old Testament and New) reveal God's rescue plan of sending his Son to suffer as the penalty for humanity's sin, thereby restoring failed relationship with God. Jesus completed his earthly ministry by giving his disciples a commission—our primary responsibility while he is gone.

In at least six places in the four Gospels and the book of Acts, Jesus directly speaks to his disciples of this responsibility. In essence, it is to go, make disciples among all ethnic groups and teach them to apply to their lives what he commanded. They're to spread the message of the glory of his kingdom and its transforming power among all ethnic groups. The Great Commission is recorded in each of the four Gospels: Matthew 28:18-20; Mark 16:14-18; Luke 24:46-49; and John 20:21-23. Jesus' words in the commission are then repeated in Acts 1:8, confirming a primary purpose for the giving of the Holy Spirit: making local and global witnesses of Jesus.

The fulfillment of the Great Commission has never been so close. What do I mean by *fulfillment*? Jesus' disciples asked him what it would be like near the end of the present age, when he would return in glory. Jesus told of a period that will be very challenging for the body of Christ. Then he spoke of the impact of the gospel and the extent of its spread in the midst of the difficulty: "And this gospel of the kingdom will be preached in all the world as a witness to all the nations, and then the end will come" (Matthew 24:14).

The word *nations* isn't an adequate translation. Jesus was not saying the gospel would be proclaimed in every geopolitical nation, but in every individual ethnic group within every nation. The Greek phrase *panta ta ethne* is where we get our term "ethnic group." You and I are part of a specific ethnic group that shares a language, traditions and so on. Statistics reveal more than sixteen thousand of these distinct groups in the world. Of those, there are more than six thousand designated as "unreached" people groups.[1] (Other terms for them include "least reached," "marginalized" or "forgotten" peoples.) An unreached people group is defined as an ethnic people among whom the indigenous community of Bible-believing followers of Jesus lacks adequate numbers and resources to evangelize and disciple the ethnic group at large.[2] Believers are usually under 2 percent of the total population.

It's also helpful to consider "unengaged" people groups, of which there are believed to be around 440. These have populations of twenty-five thousand or more and have no ministry, church or organization yet engaging them to make disciples by planting simple, indigenous, reproducing churches. In other words, there are no known believers and no churches among these ethnic groups, and the Bible isn't available in the local dialect.[3]

The *fulfillment* of the Great Commission refers to every unreached and unengaged people group receiving a living witness of Jesus. What's a witness? A presentation of the gospel that's culturally relevant and understandable to the local people and not perceived as foreign. A disciple uses bridges from the local worldview to make the gospel culturally relevant to the hearer. In this way disciples incarnate the gospel among the people as living examples of the power of Christ. A witness also includes a demonstration of power. For example, Paul's message was not with words alone but with power, verifying the authenticity of the message (Romans 15:19; 1 Corinthians 2:4-5). This power may be external (healings, miracles, other signs or wonders) or internal (deep conviction, revelation given to unbelievers regarding truth).

Though demonstrations of power aren't often considered to be important for witness in the Western world, most Majority World believers welcome the supernatural power of God, no matter their theological background. Because they come from cultures that prioritize the spirit world, they have a natural desire to operate in God's power.

Many assume that the Great Commission is for specialists or

professionals. But the fulfillment of the Great Commission requires *all* hands on deck across the body of Christ. This doesn't mean all are message bearers who leave their country for another. But all are meant to find their God-ordained role in the Great Commission, serving Jesus with all their heart. These roles include giving, advocating for unreached people groups, mobilizing others and prayer and intercession. Educating, inspiring and activating disciples in these roles is necessary to rouse the church in her calling to fulfill the Great Commission.

The fulfillment of the Great Commission requires thousands of new message bearers of high spiritual quality living among unreached and unengaged people groups. These message bearers come from historical sending nations and emerging sending nations. The spread of the gospel in the book of Acts was productive as disciples deliberately migrated to new areas, taking their work and families, with the expressed purpose of expanding the kingdom of God. Today, it's just as necessary for thousands of business owners, teachers, doctors, farmers and others to relocate their work and families to the unreached and unengaged.

The rousing of the body of Christ toward the fulfillment of the Great Commission is a deeply personal passion of mine. More than ten years ago, I was involved in founding Student Volunteer Movement 2 (SVM2) toward this end.[4] This international alliance of ministries from many organizational and denominational backgrounds develops national alliances (in primarily non-Western nations) made up of individual local ministries (churches, campus ministry fellowships and Bible schools) being transformed into "Great Commission Ministries" by implementing proven mobilization tools. Ministries are being provoked to prioritize the Great Commission and to send the "best and brightest" to the unreached and unengaged instead of keeping them back for local ministry.

The idea of the fulfillment of the Great Commission is at times condemned as a Western concept because of its goal orientation. But the non-Western church takes this goal deeply to heart, creating such exciting movements as Nigeria's Vision 50:15, with its call to raise fifty thousand Nigerian message bearers for the harvest in fifteen years, and China's Back To Jerusalem movement, which hopes to see one hundred thousand message bearers taking the gospel from China along the "Silk Road" and back to Jerusalem. The primary impetus of the AD 2000 movement of the 1980s and 1990s—to plant a church in every unreached people group by the year 2000—was instigated by the non-Western church.

Yet our motivation isn't the goal itself but obedience to our Lord's mandate to make disciples among all ethnic groups. The Bible doesn't teach that the fulfillment of the Great Commission means every person will be converted to Christ. Scripture teaches that it is at hand when God has gathered out of the world (every tribe, tongue and ethnic group) a holy and blameless body for eternal fellowship with his Son. Jesus' promise is that some from every ethnic group will take him as Savior and Lord and fellowship eternally with God in his kingdom (Revelation 7:9).

Jesus gives this commission expressly to disciples, not merely to believers. His initial call is always to himself in discipleship. The injunction of making other disciples is a given. The word *disciple* occurs in the New Testament 269 times, while *Christian* is used three times and *believer* only twice. Jesus' will is that all who call on him be true disciples. Obviously, a disciple must be a believer, but according to Jesus, not all believers are disciples.

WHAT IS A MESSAGE BEARER?

"Message bearer" is an alternative term for "sent one" or "missionary." The traditional term *missionary* carries a number of unhelpful negative stereotypes. During a ministry tour among several African and Asian nations about a decade ago, I used *missionary* regularly as I spoke to campus ministry fellowships, churches and Bible schools. But I quickly realized it was not communicating what I was intending. I met with several small groups and asked them what they thought a missionary was. None was able to capture the biblical essence. And several responses were reactions to the negative influences of colonialism. It became clear that a more effective term was needed. I asked for suggestions, and the term "message bearer" emerged. These new messengers diligently develop inner life, spiritual qualities. They're from every nation going to every nation, used of God to sow his kingdom among people who have no access to the gospel. They're committed to serving Jesus in unreached or unengaged areas through long-term, crosscultural ministry.

THE TEN ESSENTIAL SPIRITUAL KEYS

Effective message bearers have many inner-life commonalities (both historically and in contemporary circles). These are found among all disciples and not merely message bearers, yet they particularly apply to those serving Jesus in the Great Commission. I call these inner-life characteristics (which affect our actions, choices and behaviors) "spiritual keys" for thriving as God's message bearers.

Jesus' teachings highlight the importance of an inner spiritual reality, not merely external religious forms. It's difficult to pare down his teachings on this subject for a book such as this. Instead, I'll focus on *essential* spiritual keys—inner-life characteristics often neglected yet altogether necessary for thriving as God's message bearers. The neglect of one or more of these keys has led to failure among message bearers to produce eternal fruit. I'm personally challenged concerning each of these spiritual keys, and I'm committed to their ongoing development in my life. Yet they do not come easily.

What are core characteristics of spiritual equipping that enable God's message bearers to thrive in their calling among unreached and unengaged people groups? The ten essential spiritual keys are

1. being saturated with the powerful presence of God,

2. embracing humility,

3. hungering and thirsting for God,

4. being clothed with God's Word,

5. discerning God's guidance and revelation,

6. pursuing a lifestyle of prayer and fasting,

7. cooperating with God's twofold purpose,

8. understanding the times and seasons of God,

9. persevering with steadfastness and stability, and

10. pursuing a focused life.

Note the idea of growing or developing or pursuing in relation to each key. It's an act of our will to journey with Jesus in the development of each key. We spend our whole lives in this pursuit; we never "arrive." We order our lives around the cultivation of the ten spiritual keys in obedience to God. And the keys are interrelated; we can't ignore one and faithfully develop the others.

It's important to recognize that we don't earn God's love by developing spiritual keys. God's love doesn't change. It's absolute and can't be enhanced or diminished toward us. Instead, by developing spiritual keys, we prepare ourselves to be entrusted with more in God's kingdom. Out of gratitude for all God has given us, we develop the keys to produce the greatest amount of fruit for his glory.

WHO IS THIS BOOK FOR?

The essential spiritual keys are applicable to all believers who want to thrive as Jesus' disciples. They're especially helpful to those in spiritual leadership or sensing God leading in that direction—whether in a local church (pastoral and lay leadership), a campus ministry (staff or student leadership) or in a training institution or other parachurch environment.

The book's primary readership is current message bearers and those preparing to serve in the Great Commission. No matter if you have been serving in crosscultural mission for three months or thirty years, these principles will prove beneficial. Whether you're burned out or thriving, ideas and concepts in *Spiritual Equipping for Mission* will help you develop as God's message bearer. It is for members of mission sending agencies and those who provide member-care oversight, mission mobilizers, mission pastors and lay leaders, campus ministry fellowships, church college ministries, Bible and mission departments in Christian colleges and universities, student mission fellowships, seminaries and much more. It's written for Western and non-Western readers alike as we together pursue the fulfillment of the Great Commission.

AN INTENTIONAL SPIRITUAL EMPHASIS

This book's focus on the inner life and spiritual dynamics is intentional. These allow the love and power of Jesus to be released through our lives to produce the greatest measure of fruit possible. This is where the Great Commission is won or lost. Attrition (leaving the mission field for various reasons) is generally not the result of wrong ministry methods but of failing to cultivate our inner lives in God.[5]

Message bearers carefully study key missiological and cultural issues, seeking God's strategy for reaching those we're serving. We diligently study language to gain fluency within a few years.[6] Yet being equipped as fruitful message bearers primarily means developing a solid, spiritual, inner life. But, generally, this is being neglected.

THE SECRET

None of the spiritual keys are natural to any disciple; none develop on their own. Nor will God cultivate them without our commitment to the process. Each is grown as we deliberately abide in Jesus, our vine (John 15:4). Development comes as a result of time, Spirit-led effort, discipline, persistence and commitment to obeying Jesus. When we periodically fail as we develop the spiritual keys, we need to confess, receive Jesus' forgiveness, lay hold of his empowerment and press on in obedience. The message bearers who produce great fruit are those who are determined to cultivate their inner lives.

Trying harder doesn't help us grow in the spiritual keys. They grow as we allow Jesus to develop them step-by-step. We're responsible to receive his empowering by faith. We're accountable to being intentional and diligent, not letting laziness hinder us from becoming what Jesus would have us be. But ultimately the Spirit develops these spiritual keys in us as we cooperate with him.

God works over a lifetime to steadily develop the spiritual keys. So we aren't expected to have the keys before we start serving him as message bearers. God cultivates them through our successes and failures as we serve him in the nations.

1

What Is the Spirit Saying?

Many years ago, I sat in a service at my church in Pasadena, California, as a young disciple. The speaker challenged us to find what God was doing in our generation and to throw ourselves into that work. My heart was stirred! I wanted to live for God, obey him and give myself to his purposes. I wanted my life to count according to God's standards, not the world's. But I had no idea what that meant. From then on, my passion has been to discover what the Holy Spirit is saying to his church and to me personally, and to order my life around that.

To thrive as God's message bearers, we need some measure of understanding of what the Spirit is saying in the broader sense. The Holy Spirit appears to be highlighting the following points. These are not exhaustive, as the Spirit is doing much more. Yet they provide helpful foundations for our understanding of the ten spiritual keys.

OVERARCHING DYNAMIC

We will look at the following points through the lens of the Spirit's priority of wooing the body of Christ back to her first love. In Matthew 22:37, Jesus tells a lawyer that the first and greatest commandment is to love the Lord your God with all your heart, soul and mind. In Revelation 2:4, the exalted Jesus reveals to the church at Ephesus that they're a model church outwardly, effectively withstanding false teachers, but are guilty of leaving their first love.

In every generation, believers have struggled to make this first love a priority. Relating rightly with God depends on our choice to love him, and the Spirit's work is to provoke us with dynamic love for Jesus. Apart from growing in love for Jesus, it's difficult to correctly respond to the other messages the Spirit trumpets.

AWAKENING THE CHURCH

The Spirit seems to be emphasizing the need for the body of Christ to cultivate a deeper spiritual reality. In some countries, the number of believers is increasing and churches are growing, yet transformation from convert to disciple isn't keeping pace. Believers abound, but Jesus distinguishes believers from true disciples. Complacency, compromise and self-centeredness prevail. A lack of zeal to obey Jesus' commission correlates with a lack of spiritual life in the church. A lack of praying, giving, advocating, promoting, sending and going reveals the need for a revival of true and fervent devotion to Jesus and of surrender to serving him.[1] A current priority among believers should be helping revive the spiritual life of local churches and campus fellowships, that spiritual fervor for God's purposes may follow.

Those committed to global mission mostly speak about and advocate for the externals of the Great Commission: church planting, leading people to Christ, discipling others and more. This is good and right, and it's much of what I do. However, there seems to be an equally great need for promoting a deeper spiritual life. History and God's ways in Scripture reveal that helping disciples go deeper in God will, over time, motivate them to become active in his Great Commission.

JESUS' TERMS OF DISCIPLESHIP

Similarly, the Spirit seems to be promoting an alignment among believers to God's standards in Scripture. True faith isn't merely subscribing to a set of doctrinal ideas. It involves being born again from above and ordering our lives around obeying the will of God revealed through his Word. Though he has ever-flowing mercy and grace for our weakness, he will not compromise the conditions for how his people should live, as set forth in Scripture by divine wisdom.

Yes, we are saved by grace and simple faith in the shed blood of Christ. The Son of God is the only sacrifice able to make us clean from our inherent waywardness. Nothing we do makes us more "qualified" for salvation. However, cooperating with God as a fruitful, Spirit-empowered disciple requires daily choices, prioritizing our lives around God's kingdom (Matthew 6:33).

Jesus called his disciples to follow wholeheartedly or not at all. Why would he do this? We find an answer in Luke 14:25-33. Jesus tells the crowds, "You can't be my disciples" apart from embracing loyalty (v. 26), denying self (v. 27) and forsaking all we have (v. 33). Yet everything in us protests the severity of such terms. We wonder why we're expected to meet these seemingly impossible standards.

Jesus provides the answer through two illustrations in verses 28-32: (1) a builder considering the necessary materials before building a tower and (2) a king preparing for war by evaluating the quality of his soldiers. We often call this "counting the cost" of following Jesus. And though it's edifying to interpret the verses this way, Jesus seems to have been teaching something altogether different. The cost isn't ours to count but Jesus', as he takes inventory of the body of Christ. He counts the cost to see if *he* has adequate materials to complete a building. It isn't we who are a king going to war and considering the quality of the soldiers, but Jesus evaluating our quality for the battle.

Jesus' illustrations highlight two operations of his work in the earth: construction and war. He is in the world to build and to battle. But what did he mean by this? Jesus is consumed with a desire to manifest his kingdom. To build effectively, he first considers the "materials." To win the battle, he considers his army and its quality before setting off to war. His standards are high, because he has much invested in us (disciples) as coheirs and coworkers with him. Jesus has redeemed the body of Christ at the cost of his own blood for building and battling with him. When we understand these principles, we recognize the wisdom of his seemingly high standards.

God doesn't require such standards without enabling his people to walk the standards out. Doing so would be cruel. He would be teasing us if, in our humanity, we could never actually walk in the commands and teachings of Scripture. Instead, Jesus' death and resurrection and the Spirit's enabling are sufficient for us to align with his terms of discipleship. We obtain these spiritual resources through receiving his empowering in every circumstance. This enables our growing effectiveness in the Great Commission.

ALIGNING WITH GOD'S ETERNAL HEART

The totality of the Bible reveals God as a "missionary" God. And the Spirit seems to be provoking individuals, denominations, churches, campus ministry fellowships, Christian colleges, small groups and individual believers to align with the will of God (Matthew 7:21; Mark 3:34-35). The Lord is calling people from every ethnic group to love and obey the Father. He's fulfilling the global purposes on his heart from the foundations of the world. He's moved with eternal love to restore humanity to life as it was meant to be lived—in obedience to his ways as revealed in Scripture.

Over the past twenty years, there has been an unprecedented turning to faith in Christ around the world, especially in China, Latin America, Africa and parts of Asia.[2] This awakening is the firstfruits of what the Lord will bring in coming decades. A global harvest is on the horizon, coming from the least-reached places on earth. And the Lord is orchestrating events to prepare for such an increase.

God receives the greatest amount of honor and glory when men and women, boys and girls are restored to his eternal purpose of rightly fellowshiping with him. They're forever changed, freed from the shackles of compulsion to sin. They progress in spiritual maturity, and they are marked by obedience to God's standards, self-denial and love. This transformation is the work of the Spirit.

MY OWN STORY

Because I'm a fourth-generation message bearer, I've had these truths imprinted on me throughout my life. My paternal great-grandparents served in India, and my grandparents were also in India and later the Philippines. My parents served in Papua New Guinea with Wycliffe Bible Translators. I was born in New Guinea and lived the first seven years of life there.

Though I had the seeds of God's burning heart for the world sown in my heart in early childhood, they did not come to fruition until much later. As a seventeen-year-old, I sensed God leading me toward involvement in ministry. My family had long since returned to the United States from New Guinea when my dad became a professor at Fuller Seminary in Pasadena, California. I had a hunger for God as a teenager and was involved in leadership in my high school youth group. But because of my heritage (and my pride), I wanted to chart a different course than my family.

I made a deal with God that I would serve him in any way he wanted—as long as it was in America. But I found out quickly that it isn't wise to make such deals with God. He orchestrated many events between my first and third years at Azusa Pacific University in Southern California, pointing me toward serving him in cross-cultural mission.

I had a choice to make. Would I obey or ignore the gentle leading of the Spirit? When I was nineteen, I prayed a simple prayer of surrender to this growing conviction: "Jesus, I'm willing that you make me willing!" In doing so, I didn't overlook that I needed his passion inside my heart for the nations. By the time I was twenty-one, God had started me on the course of serving him in the Great Commission; he had stirred my heart with his own passion. Though I had no idea where the road would lead, I was surrendered to his will.

BECOMING A DWELLING PLACE

The first-century church understood Jesus' purpose being done through them, and more importantly, they possessed the means of seeing that vision accomplished. They were a dwelling place of God's presence. This meant God's presence among them was more than doctrinal truth, but also experiential reality. It's the same for us as the Spirit beckons us to offer ourselves to Jesus, giving him his rightful place. It's the call of Romans 12:1-2:

> I beseech you therefore, brethren, by the mercies of God, that you present your bodies a living sacrifice, holy, acceptable to God, which is your reasonable service. And do not be conformed to this world, but be transformed by the renewing of your mind, that you may prove what is that good and acceptable and perfect will of God.

In this process of becoming a dwelling place of God, a primary work of the Spirit is ridding us of the self life.[3] It isn't what we do for him that counts. The offering God delights in is our willingness to die in increasing measure to the invasive self life (Romans 6:11) and to grow in love for him. The depth to which we're willing to die to ourselves is the height to which God will use us for his glory.

Cain's and Abel's offerings in Genesis 4:3-5 demonstrate this principle. God was pleased with Abel's offering but not with Cain's. Why? Abel's offering was according to God's terms of accomplishing salvation through the blood of sacrifice (Hebrews 12:24). Cain sought to please God and gain his acceptance through producing something with his own hands. We find this dichotomy across the body of Christ. We are all naturally Cains, yet God is seeking to transform us into Abels.

Abel understood he could not please God in his own capacity, while Cain believed his actions were good enough for God. Christ's sacrificial death is all we need for salvation. In gratitude, we choose to become like him through dying more and more to ourselves. This is what Paul meant when he taught, "Present your bodies a living sacrifice" as well as when he affirmed, "I die daily" (1 Corinthians 15:31). Through this process of dying, God is able to fill us (by degrees) with his own life. In this way we become a dwelling place of God.

Our vision is clear: to be a people "who [turn] the world upside down" by abiding with Jesus and being filled with his divine life (Acts 17:6). We receive his overcoming life within by faith and are activated to work toward an increasing measure of the kingdom of God among universities, cities, villages, peoples and nations who today are hostile to or have not yet heard of Jesus.

THE GREAT EXCHANGE

Near the beginning of his ministry, the great American evangelist of the late 1800s, D. L. Moody, reportedly heard a friend comment, "The world has yet to see what God will do through a person fully consecrated to him."[4] Moody said to his friend, "By the Holy Spirit in me, I will be that man!" Throughout history, few disciples have been fully consecrated to God (surrendered to his leadership). The Spirit is motivating believers all over the world toward such wholehearted surrender.

God desires that we exchange our lives for the forming of Christ within us. A simple prayer I often pray is "All I am for all that he is!" The vision of God for every human being is his Son formed within us. We willingly surrender control to his capable hands and in exchange receive more of his fullness within. We do so with the awareness that in us "nothing good dwells" (Romans 7:18). We embrace frailty and weakness, receiving instead the life and power of Jesus.

King David is our example. He "served his own generation by the will of God" (Acts 13:36). He was acquainted with brokenness and weakness, and prone to sin—just like us. He was called a "man after God's own heart" because of his commitment to turn back to God each time he failed, doing whatever was necessary to reconcile his life with God. Though David had many flaws, God saw his passion to walk with him in love and obedience.

In Acts 13:22, Paul spoke of God's thought about David: "[God] raised up for them David as king, to whom also He gave testimony and said, 'I have found David the son of Jesse, a man after My own heart, who will do all My will.'" God said David would "do all My will." How could he say this when we know David made costly mistakes? Because God sees things differently than we do. He sees a man who is weak yet with heartfelt, genuine sincerity turns from waywardness quickly and obeys.

COOPERATING WITH GOD

God is sovereign, ruling over history, the present and the future. Yet he has set up his kingdom so its primary means of advance is through the voluntary global church. God has chosen, out of love, to limit himself. He doesn't *need* us, but out of deep love, he has set up his kingdom in partnership with weak and broken disciples. One of the Spirit's fundamental roles is enabling us to cooperate with God, which is essential to equipping the body of Christ for mission.

Some see God's will determined solely by his sovereignty; in doing this, they relinquish their ordained role in partnership with him. His foreknowledge is perfect, as he is acquainted with the future and all that will happen. And in his sovereignty, God has determined primary events. This doesn't mean, however, that we don't have choices to make. Nothing is so predestined that God's will alone is steering history; the choices we make along the way matter. They reveal how responsive we are to God. Through them we chart a course, and God leads and guides according to his will.

God gives choices to provide dignity. He wants loyal followers, not programmed robots. Voluntary participation in the Great Commission is one of those choices. The eternity he has placed in our hearts causes us to long to participate with God in what is of the utmost eternal significance (Ecclesiastes 3:11). We were created to cooperate with him as he works out his plans and purposes in the earth.

The extraordinary fact is that God will bring about the fulfillment of the Great Commission without violating the free will of people. We can say no to cooperation with God and still be saved. Paul speaks of these types of believers in 1 Corinthians 3:15: "If anyone's work is burned, he will suffer loss; but he himself will be saved, yet so as through fire." Paul's focus here is on believers appearing before the judgment seat of Christ having wasted their lives in self-centered pursuits. Every believer will undergo this judgment when Jesus takes inventory of our lives. It's an evaluation not related to eternal punishment but to rewards distributed on the basis of loving God and doing his will.[5] Though works do not save us, they're a basis by which we will be evaluated.

Such cooperation with God doesn't come without opposition. History confirms that the greatest in-gatherings of people to faith have been amid difficult conditions. Two examples are the first-century church under the Roman Empire and the church in modern

China under communism. Both saw multitudes drawn into the kingdom of God under oppressive governmental regimes. And only those who truly encountered the Lord and joined the community of faith from pure motives faithfully endured. This kept the church vibrant, as believers were forced to count the cost of following Jesus.

The kingdom is in raging conflict with forces of darkness, and it often appears to suffer defeat. It faces opposition at every corner. Simultaneously, disciples provide a witness of Christ, cooperating with God in the fulfillment of the Great Commission. Even now, evil seems to be increasing as Satan rages against Jesus and the body of Christ. Though darkness is getting darker, light is also increasing to a stunning brightness. We're entering days of *great* global harvest—and *terrible* intensifying pressure. The Spirit is being unleashed among unreached and unengaged people groups, using ordinary and weak believers like you and me as we respond to God's call to cooperation.

THE SEARCH

The Spirit is orchestrating a divine search all over the earth: "For the eyes of the LORD run to and fro throughout the whole earth, to show Himself strong on behalf of those whose heart is loyal to Him" (2 Chronicles 16:9). God's search is unlike any the world has known; it's based on a completely different set of criteria. He searches for those who will abandon every competing allegiance to their loyalty to Jesus in a surrendered response of love, as bond slaves to God, who has bought and owns them (1 Corinthians 6:19-20).

Today we're witnessing great shifts in the way the global church functions, expresses itself and is led. The Global South (the nations across Latin America, Africa and Asia, primarily in the southern hemisphere) is now the center of vibrant Christianity and is gaining momentum as a sender. Indigenous national churches in historically "mission receiving" countries are now sending message bearers to the unreached and unengaged. This includes those in sub-Saharan Africa, South America and Asia. God is finding and empowering thousands whom others might overlook and write off.

First Samuel 16:7 reminds us, "The Lord does not see as man sees, . . . but the Lord looks at the heart." God's search overlooks a person's family, education, personality type, natural abilities, sociability, inadequacy, past failings, former sin, age, gender, financial status, physical appearance and ethnicity. His search considers the responses of a person's heart toward his or her king. The heart is the wellspring of life. Those bent on genuine love for Jesus allow the Spirit to refine them and equip them as servants among the nations.

God searches for those who value growing intimacy with Jesus, those who will be trustworthy with the secrets of his heart. He seeks those embracing a life of faith and dependence on him. He pursues those ignoring what others say while living according to Jesus' standards. He beckons those disillusioned with the status quo, dreaming with God about what could be. He looks for those using time, money, gifts, abilities and influence to advance his kingdom. This search is a priority of the Spirit as he partners with the body of Christ in fulfilling the Great Commission.

2

Being Saturated with the
Powerful Presence of God

Spiritual Key # 1

Perhaps no other factor contributes more to the ability to produce spiritual fruit than God's powerful presence in a life. A human life filled with the presence and power of God is one of God's choicest gifts to his church and the world.[1] Because our first spiritual key—being saturated with God's presence—is a combination of several other keys and is necessary for their development, we'll explore it first.

WHAT DO WE MEAN BY SATURATED?

Bobby Clinton, one of my professors at Fuller Seminary, says, "The essential ingredient of [spiritual] leadership is the powerful presence of God in the leaders' life and ministry."[2] This is true of leadership in general as well as of every disciple responding to Jesus' Great Commission. Our personalities, words and daily activities can become filled with God's power and authority, though we may feel weak. For us to be saturated with God's powerful presence, Jesus must possess our being through the Spirit. This involves learning, through trial and error, to walk obediently in his ways. The authoritative life of Jesus within us must be given its rightful place. His presence through us proves the faithfulness of God before an unbelieving world and an often skeptical church.

I remember sitting in Bobby's class when the weight of these truths got ahold of me. Spiritual leadership in crosscultural ministry is about walking with God, who fills us with himself. No longer did I need to strive in ministry. Instead, as I was faithful and obedient to cultivate depth with Jesus, he would reveal himself through my life. I understood that to live this way required a whole new mind-set and approach. (Many of the keys in this book involve the habits I needed to develop.)

The opposite of being saturated with the presence of God as a message bearer is operating in ministry from our own strength, relying on our natural abilities, skills and strengths. By nature we're capable and strong, able to plan, to think and to accomplish. In contrast, God wants us serving from a place of voluntary weakness, where we don't think or plan apart from him. We may be working hard, sacrificing and doing a great deal. And others may say we're doing a great work, yet there is something lacking. There is little to no real spirituality.[3] We're spiritually barren. To avoid this all-too-common problem, I find it helpful to do periodic self-exams, asking the Lord if my work is being done more in the power of the flesh or the Spirit.

Jacob is a picture of the difference between operating from the natural life and operating in reliance on the Lord (see Genesis 27–33). Before the angel wrestled with him by the River Jabbok, Jacob was a schemer, manipulator and conniver. He was smart and confident in himself. As it is with many of us, Jacob's desires were right (to do the will of God), but his means of attaining those desires were wrong. Human ingenuity and strength doesn't accomplish the will of God. So God confronted Jacob, giving him a limp and turning him into another man, free from natural striving and strength, yielded to the power of God's presence in and through him.

The world, our self-dependent natures and the enemy make us

less dependent on Jesus in our lives and ministries. Paul wrote of this problem in Galatians 3:3: "Having begun in the Spirit, are you now being made perfect by the flesh?" In many of the Epistles, especially Galatians and Corinthians, Paul reveals the one reason behind the church's general low state: many are living in the power of the flesh. They began well in their life of faith by receiving the Spirit. But as time went on, they tried to build on the work of the Spirit through their own effort. Message bearers are called to live in the power of the Spirit but often live in the power of the flesh and self-will. This is true in our spiritual lives as well as in the outworkings of ministry. It's easy to become reliant on ministry skill and ability instead of on God's presence.

In my early thirties, I fell into this trap. I had learned to speak relatively well while becoming good at the various tasks related to our SVM2 work. And I had slowly become dependent on these skills instead of God. My fellowship with Jesus began to dry up as I was busy with "ministry." One morning it hit me how much I was doing for God in human power, with little awareness of him. This appalled me, and I quickly repented, turning back to God. I now know that, ultimately, it's Jesus' life within mine that produces true spiritual influence that stands the test of time.

THE LORD WAS WITH THEM

One condition for producing fruit in God's kingdom repeatedly shows up in Scripture and in mission history, though it's phrased in more than one way: "The Lord was with them," "The hand of the Lord was upon them," "The power of the Spirit rested on them," "They were filled with the Spirit" and so on. This is a power-packed spiritual key. In Scripture, we're rarely told of a biblical character's personal charm, great oratorical abilities or skills in drawing a crowd. God purposely looks beyond these qualities to focus on the one essential ingredient to kingdom effectiveness: a life saturated with his powerful presence.

Joseph's remarkable life, highlighted in Genesis 37–50, teaches this spiritual key. Scripture says in four different places, "the Lord was with Joseph" (saturating him with God's presence). Though Joseph encountered hardship, the Bible doesn't have one negative word to say about him. Joseph graduated from one test to another as he responded with faithfulness to God. And in the midst of challenges, he didn't get offended at God.

Joseph's life teaches that difficulties are God's testing ground for what he has created us to walk in. And message bearers experience them often: visa problems, local opposition, backlashes to our witness, not enough funds or people to do the work. How we respond reveals much about us. As God sees our faithfulness in small areas, he expands us in relation to those areas. At each step he continues to watch. As we're faithful and obedient, he releases increasing measures of his powerful presence within us.

At this moment, we're in God's school of testing. In fact, our whole lives could be considered that. He's watching our hearts, conversations, prayer lives, motives, words and eyes, and how we use our time, money and abilities. His watching isn't motivated by a desire to scrutinize but by a heart of delight in relationship with us, as he woos us to walk in ways we were created for.

Several years ago, I was praying about upcoming ministry plans in India. One morning, during a time of personal prayer, the Lord spoke to me not to contact two leaders related to those plans; he gave me their names. I was faithful for a few days, but I started feeling pressure to make headway. I thought those two leaders were keys to helping break a logjam, so I went ahead and contacted them, disregarding God's leading. Over the following days, I experienced a marked difference in my spirit. It was not guilt (though there was some of that) but difficulty sensing the powerful presence of Jesus within me and on my work. I had grieved the Spirit. He had tested my ability to hear his voice and obey, and I had failed. I quickly realized this and repented, turning back to God in obedience.

MOSES' AND JOSHUA'S CRIES

Serving God in the Great Commission means declaring what Moses prayed so long ago: "If Your Presence does not go with us, do not bring us up from here!" (Exodus 33:15). When he prayed this, God was leading him to take the Israelites into the Promised Land. Moses, aware of his limitations and his inability to accomplish such a feat in his own power, cried out to God to remember promising to bring his people into the Promised Land. Moses then asked God to accompany his own woefully inadequate attempts with his powerful presence.

Moses knew the correct posture to have when serving God. Like him, we feel inadequate, ill-prepared, too weak and broken to produce any fruit for God's kingdom. Jesus knows our weakness; he knows our inability to produce anything of our own accord. This is why he promises his powerful presence to us. It's his presence that brings fruitfulness, his presence that makes a way.

We find the statement "I will be with you" spoken to Joshua as he prepared to take over leadership of the Israelites after Moses' death. Moses was a legendary leader, and Joshua must have been overwhelmed to take the reins from this giant. He obviously was insecure about how he would be received and if he would live up to the expectations placed on him by others, himself and the position he was filling. In Joshua 1:5-9, God assured Joshua of his presence and announced four times in five verses that Joshua was to be "strong and courageous" as a result. God was stamping this message of being strong and courageous onto Joshua's insecure spirit.

God shows no partiality. What he did with those in the Bible he does with us. He's the same God who was with Joseph, Moses and Joshua. We can expect him to be with us too as we obediently align with the conditions of his Word.

JESUS' WORDS IN THE GREAT COMMISSION

Matthew 28:18-20 is the most famous Great Commission passage. Jesus qualifies his call to *go* and disciple the nations (*panta ta ethne*—ethnic people groups), clarifying first the authority by which his followers would do his work. Jesus emphasizes that as a result of his obedience on the cross, he has obtained all authority in heaven and on earth forever. Based on this fact, he instructs his disciples to go and make disciples.

The implication is that as disciples are faithful to God's global mandate, the same authority will be delegated to them. Great spiritual authority is available to those seeking the expansion of the kingdom of God, doing the will of the Father. To those obeying the Great Commission mandate, Jesus promises, "I will be with you." As we make it our life's ambition to bring Jesus glory through making disciples of all ethnic groups, we can be sure his powerful presence will be upon us.

EXAMPLES AND CHARACTERISTICS

In Mauritania, a Muslim country hostile to the gospel, a friend and his family served the poorest of the poor for over twenty years. They yielded to the Lord to be saturated with his powerful presence, and they saw tremendous results among the people. A practice they developed early was to make sure that, within the first three minutes of every conversation with a new person, he or she knew they were followers of Jesus and where they could be found. This practice had obvious risks yet proved fruitful, as many inquirers who otherwise would not have known where to speak to a follower of Jesus sought them out. These message bearers operated in boldness, which is a characteristic of those saturated with the powerful presence of God.

David Brainerd, a message bearer among American Indians in the area of Pennsylvania and New Jersey during the 1730s, became saturated with God's powerful presence.[4] He served several years among the Indians with little to nothing to show for it. He was prone to spiritual and emotional highs and lows, and he fought illness constantly. After many changes in location, Brainerd settled with a tribe in New Jersey. After seasons devoted to intense intercessory prayer, a spiritual awakening arose, greatly affecting the Indians. During those seasons of prayer, Brainerd would at times come under intense travail and anguish for souls. He would be gripped by a power enabling him to stand in the gap for whole days for the Indians. When he preached to the Indians, great conviction fell as they repented of sin, embracing Jesus as the true God. This fruit stuck as the tribe continued walking in the Lord, guiding their children in Jesus for generations. Intense intercessory prayer for souls is a characteristic of those saturated with the presence of God.

Mary Slessor, a single Scottish woman who went in the 1870s to Calibar in modern southern Nigeria, was also of this sort.[5] Life as a message bearer was lonely and difficult for her. Through trials, hardships and physical weakness, she remained faithful to Jesus. The tribal religion abounded with witchcraft, and the people saw twins as a curse; in most situations, both babies were murdered. Mary, saturated with the presence of God, was a tool of God's justice through rescuing the babies, ministering to the mothers and standing against the witch doctors who perpetrated the fear.[6]

I have several close Nigerian friends who are twins. They look with gratitude at Mary's legacy of being used of God to put away this horrible act of murder. Doing God's works of justice is a characteristic of those saturated with the presence of God.

I was recently in the West African nation of Guinea. A similarly engrained cultural tradition continues to brutalize many ethnic groups in this region and elsewhere in sub-Saharan Africa: female circumcision. It's believed a woman isn't a real woman unless circumcised, ridding her of sexual desire. The motivation for this practice, rooted in Islamic tradition, is to keep teenage girls virginal until married, by taking away sexual sensations. It's also said that circumcision protects married women from desire and subsequently from overwhelming their husbands, as they will have two or three other wives as well.

Women are the main encouragers of this practice, which makes sense culturally. If your daughter isn't considered a woman by society, of course you want her to follow the traditions required for her to become a "woman." However, this is a denial of God's creation of woman as a sexual being in the confines of a loving marriage. It's a practice needing modern Mary Slessors saturated with the powerful presence of God and lifting voices of truth against the onslaught of cultural lies.

THE POWER OF BIOGRAPHIES

Have you noticed how much of the Bible is written as biography? We read about Abraham, Jacob, Moses, Ruth, Joshua, Samuel, the kings, Esther, Daniel, Jesus, Peter, Paul and more. We're meant to look on others' lives, letting their strengths and weaknesses shine light on our own. The positive examples are a witness of what is possible in God; they provide a Spirit-empowered motivation to pursue similar goals. The negative examples are warnings to avoid making their mistakes.[7]

I try to read a biography every three or four months. This stretches my vision of God and ignites passion to know him deeper, while revealing the variety of ways he might want to use me in ministry. A principle in biographies is "like attracts like." We're often attracted to the biography of someone with a purpose in God similar to our own. Something about their life touches us. God used a biography I read almost twenty years ago to set me on the ministry course I'm on today: *Is That Really You, God?* by Loren Cunningham about the founding of YWAM.[8] Other biographies have also deeply impacted me:

- John R. Mott (missionary statesman)

- Hudson Taylor (pioneer missionary in China)

- Oswald Chambers (author)

- Andrew Murray (pastor and author)

- John Sung (Chinese revivalist)

- Praying Hyde (missionary intercessor in India)

- Count Zinzendorf (Moravian leader and missionary statesman)[9]

As we read biographies we're motivated to move to a higher spiritual level. Something inspires us to imitate the person during a particular season. When this happens to you, don't just continue reading. Stop, talk to the Lord about the area highlighted and commit yourself to walking in a new and different way. This has happened to me many times through a host of biographies of men and women who served God well. My eyes are lifted to see living examples of being saturated with God's presence.

WALKING IN GOD'S POWERFUL PRESENCE

Being saturated with God's presence is not about abilities, skills, personalities or temperaments. Those becoming saturated experience the presence of God in their daily lives. They walk with God, finding him a present help in time of need. They prove his goodness by seeing his promises in Scripture brought into experience. They unlock God's mysteries using the key of faith and open God's vast treasure chest by the means of prayer. This doesn't necessarily happen every day, nor do they feel victorious all the time. But the overall bent of their lives is in this direction. These disciples demonstrate to a watching world that "He is a rewarder of those who diligently seek him" (Hebrews 11:6).

It can be discouraging to look at this list of qualities and conclude, "I am not like this, so why try?" Remember, this doesn't happen overnight. And remember that historic figures known today as great men and women of God were normal people. They grew in spiritual depth, increasing their capacities to receive from God and applying this to their ministries. Then, at crucial moments, he used them for great things. Our daily responsibility is to faithfully journey in becoming saturated with more of God's powerful presence.

God's use of historic figures was not only in public ways, however. The chronicles of heaven will reveal multitudes of great men and women of God saturated with the presence of God and used for incredible things that the public never knew about.

Most message bearers have been sincere, with a motivation to serve God. Yet sincerity alone doesn't result in being saturated. It's common to find message bearers hoping to walk in God's power apart from aligning with his conditions. However, God has scripturally based means of releasing his kingdom authority through disciples. We must deliberately study God's ways, precepts and commands—then apply them.

GOD'S CALLING

The apostle Paul was getting at this concept in Philippians 3:12: "But I press on, that I may lay hold of that which Christ Jesus has also laid hold of me." I've taken this text as a life verse. It reveals an important element of serving God: receiving his strength. I seek to "do" this verse while simultaneously helping others "lay hold."

Paul understood there was a twofold calling on his life. First, he was called to live in a growing relationship with Jesus. He was to experience in Jesus a fountain of wisdom, understanding and revelation concerning God and his ways. This was Paul's central passion. Second, Paul was to do great works for God's kingdom. This was possible because of Christ's empowering through his death and resurrection. Grasping the multitude of ways Christ had laid hold of him was crucial to Paul's right response. In gratitude, he sought to bring Jesus the greatest amount of glory possible.

For Paul, becoming saturated with God's powerful presence meant emptying himself and receiving more of the Spirit, whose work within any individual brings eternal fruit (both inward and outward). Paul knew it was possible to come up short in walking out his calling. This motivated him to continually "lay hold" of the spiritual resources for which Jesus had "laid hold" of him.

"Laying hold" includes confidence in the Lord's commissioning in ministry. We do not put ourselves into a ministry of our own accord but rely on Jesus' appointing to a particular work. Paul was confident it was not human will but God's he was serving. Serving out of human will is common. Our intentions to serve God are sincere and genuine, and our churches, organizations and leaders appoint us. This is how God works, but we must be confident it isn't people but God appointing us. Without this confidence, message bearers can struggle to persevere during challenging days. And sometimes they find something easier to do for God.

The assurance that God has appointed us to a work relieves ministry pressure. If we are serving of our own human will, pressure to maintain a ministry is constant. Conversely, if we are confident God has put us in a ministry, there's freedom to trust him to make sure his will is done through that ministry. This frees us from nagging anxiety and worry about maintaining a ministry through human strength. We still work hard, but from the source of God's strength and power, not our own.

God wants disciples to grow in the same calling as Paul. Of course, he had a particular apostolic purpose. But the injunction to "lay hold" doesn't focus on the form our labor takes. Deepening our grasp of the ways Christ has laid hold of us and the subsequent "laying hold" in whatever sphere God gives us is our calling, no matter the type of work.

Through Christ's work, a banqueting table of divine resources has been set for message bearers. We desperately need these resources, yet we're often unaware they exist or too self-sufficient to know we need them. As with Paul, it's our prerogative how much we're willing to apply them to our lives and ministries. Paul shows us that "laying hold" for God in ministry has a dynamic connection to how close we are to Jesus. There are deeper levels of divine enabling available to bring God glory among the nations.

CHARACTERISTICS

Message bearers becoming saturated in God's powerful presence seek him in deeper dimensions, declaring through their lives that Jesus is who he says he is and can be trusted. We can choose to receive or reject this saturation. Again, this has no bearing on our eternal salvation but on experiencing the awakened spiritual life God intends us to operate in.

If God is forming Jesus within us, isn't it conceivable that he may require of us certain acts of obedience others might not be subject to? He won't let us manipulate, scheme or push ourselves forward, while others seem to do so without restriction. He requires us to die to self while others seem to parade about, getting much attention. Others may come into large amounts of money, while we may not. He may even allow others to be given credit for something we accomplished.[10]

God's presence is the indispensable component for producing fruit in the nations. To see movements to Christ among unreached and unengaged people groups, we need more of his presence operating in and through us. True spiritual authority isn't natural. No human can influence another toward spiritual understanding without God's powerful presence intervening. As message bearers, we know how inadequate we are, so our hearts yearn for a greater measure of God's presence working through us to bring forth fruit.

In Isaiah 11:2, we find seven additions the Holy Spirit provides: "The Spirit of the LORD shall rest upon Him, the Spirit of wisdom and understanding, the Spirit of counsel and might, the Spirit of knowledge and the fear of the LORD." Seven is the number of completeness. These are seven facets of what the Spirit does, making up the completeness of who he is. These seven are spoken about Jesus and, by delegation, about disciples saturated with his presence. We want to become aware of these seven areas of the Spirit's work and deliberately seek to grow in them.

What does God's presence saturating his people look like? What does it add to a life? Consider the following instances:

- A Filipino struggling to obey Jesus or his boss develops sacrificial love for Jesus, choosing to obey him.

- A Malaysian understands God's love intellectually, and through seeking God experiences that love deep in her heart.

- An Argentine yearns to experience what he knows about Jesus in his personal situtations. The Lord opens his eyes to how he's working behind the scenes in his life.

- A South African is timid, unsure of herself. She aligns with God's conditions of becoming saturated and speaks with boldness to many on campus.

- A Chinese man isn't sure how to proceed in ministry. He discerns God's leading during prayer and the next day takes steps of faith.

- A Brit needs visa papers in a hurry and seeks Jesus for favor. God's answer comes: an immigration officer calls after having previously denied him.

- A Mexican has struggled with his questionable character. Over time, as he grows in Jesus, inner-life fruit becomes apparent.

- A Kenyan serves in a people group with no running water. She fights the temptation to quit, and God gives her courage to face the challenge with joy.

- A Canadian loves Jesus and has struggled with an addiction to pornography. As he submits to the saturating of God's presence, spiritual strength is provided to overcome each new temptation.

- An Australian is confused by a difficult situation she is facing. After she spends time in the Word, God gives insight to interpret the situation according to his will.

- A Singaporean is praying for a friend but unsure how to pray. She asks the Lord to show her how to pray and waits for an answer. God puts thoughts into her mind she had never considered praying for her friend.

- A Ugandan forgets the directions to the village he's ministering to. While on a road, he hears the still, small voice of Jesus leading him along.

- An Indian becomes aware that the evil one is seeking to harm him in a particular way. The Lord shows him how to overcome that specific fiery dart.

- An American is treated with disrespect, and her anger rises. Instead of getting even, she uses the opportunity to embrace meekness.

- A Brazilian teaches that Jesus is superior to all other gods. He prays, and miracles happen, testifying to Jesus' supremacy.

- A German is struggling relationally with those on her ministry team. Though she's tempted to quit because of their differences, God fills her with abounding love.

- An Indonesian has been faithful to God in a particular ministry for twenty years. God gives strength, vision and clarity for the next season, moving him toward his ongoing, God-ordained destiny.

MORAL PURITY

Many areas hinder God's powerful presence in our lives. One is failure to walk in moral purity. Sexual immorality opens human beings to many negative spiritual influences. It hinders our sensitivity to God, numbing our hearts and spiritual capacities. God created us to enjoy sexuality in the confines of a loving, committed relationship between husband and wife. Pursuing our needs elsewhere is a recipe for disaster.

Genesis 39 reveals the practical importance of moral purity. In it, Potiphar's wife aggressively seeks to seduce Joseph. She's a picture of the onslaught of sexual temptation against the people of God. Conversely, Joseph is a picture of standing faithfully against the onslaught, come what may. As we remain faithful as Jesus' disciples, overcoming orchestrated schemes of darkness, we follow Joseph's lead. A disciple continually stumbling in sexual sin without gaining victory has a difficult time cultivating the presence of God.

A young couple went to serve in Turkey. The first step in most crosscultural ministry situations is learning the local language, so they began working with a male Turkish language tutor together. After a few weeks, it proved difficult to continue together, as the two of them were developing in their language skill at different paces. They began to meet individually with the tutor for study. After some weeks, the wife began sleeping with the Turkish man, unbeknownst to her young husband. This illicit relationship went on for several months. One day he returned home earlier than expected to find them together.

In 2011, as my family and I were preparing to relocate from Turkey to Thailand, a good friend and mission leader commented, "Be very careful in Thailand, as it has chewed up and spit out a large number of workers." He was referring to sexual temptations too often succumbed to by message bearers.

Such accounts aren't uncommon in mission. The new cultural

environment often takes its toll in unexpected ways. For some, this produces less resistance to sexual temptation. Without the support structures found within home cultures, the ease of falling into sin becomes difficult to overcome. So it's important to implement protective safeguards. Make yourself vulnerable to an accountability partner. Don't go to places or be with people with whom temptation is accentuated. Above all, bring your temptation to Jesus and receive his overcoming grace with each tempting situation you face.

The account of Joseph and Potiphar's wife teaches right motivation in relation to purity. In Genesis 39:9, Joseph responded to her, "How can I do this great wickedness, and sin against God?" Joseph understood the connection between walking intimately with God and living saturated with his powerful presence. Sinning against God would break that intimate fellowship, and Joseph couldn't bear that thought. Joseph valued God's presence more than the enticements of sin. But why do we protect ourselves from succumbing to sexual impurity? Too often, it is to maintain our reputation: if we fall, it will negatively affect how others view us, and we will hurt our family. This is certainly a good and powerful motivation, but is it the biblical motivation?

Joseph was motivated by his bond with God and by the devastating effects willful sin would have on that bond. He loved God—his presence, intimacy, ways and fellowship. The thought of losing that for a night of pleasure was unthinkable to Joseph. In the Old Testament, this is often referred to as the "fear of the Lord." We're "fearful" of severing intimate relationship with God and the blessing this bond elicits. Sin is detrimental, as it cuts us off from God's powerful presence. The fear of the Lord is an awareness of our inability to love and serve God apart from his presence operating within us. It is meant to motivate us to walk uprightly before the Lord. We realize that nothing is as important as intimate fellowship with Jesus cultivating his powerful presence in our lives.

ABIDING: THE DOORWAY TO BECOMING SATURATED

How can we be saturated with God's powerful presence? The answer is simple—yet living it is quite challenging. We abide in Jesus (John 15:4-5), spending long hours with him—enjoying intimate fellowship, resting in him, gazing on his beauty and meditating on his personhood and works. We give ourselves to open adoration, unhindered worship and gratitude for who he is and the divine purposes he's working on earth.

Jesus began teaching me this lesson of abiding when I was a nineteen-year-old student at Azusa Pacific. He took me through a period of spiritual awakening that lasted about six months. As I sought God's face, he poured his Spirit on me in a way I had not previously known. A powerful desire (not conjured in my own strength) to simply "be" with Jesus consumed me. I didn't want to attend classes, spend time with friends or be entertained. I simply wanted to abide with Jesus, fellowshiping with him. I spent hours each day in prayer and reading the Bible without getting bored or looking at my watch. Time flew by as God brought the Bible to life, teaching me spiritual concepts I had not previously known. He was stamping on me the importance of abiding in Christ in a way I've not forgotten.

Abiding in Jesus is a doorway to becoming saturated with God's powerful presence. It connects us more with his heart, producing an increased measure of his presence in us. Having this capacity expanded is an ongoing process. There are no shortcuts. We're meant to go deep with Jesus in costly devotion. We experience his presence in our hearts, minds and spirits while releasing it on others through our lives and ministries. Our watchword echoes the apostle Paul's "that I may know Him" (Philippians 3:10), and other desires become secondary. He is our priority, and loving, obeying and glorifying him is our life's ambition.

MATURING OUR TRUST

When I was a twenty-year-old student at Azusa Pacific, the Lord taught me a lesson in trusting him. I had been living on campus in an apartment for two years with friends. While in prayer, I sensed God asking me to live at home with my parents during the next year instead of continuing to live on campus. There was no logical reason that I could see for doing so, but I chose to obey. A few years later, the Lord reminded me of that situation, and he showed me it was a test to see my level of trust. Would I obey when I didn't understand why? He also reminded me how events in the intervening years had been connected to my willingness to obey and live at home.

Jeremiah 17:5-10 teaches us the importance of maturing in trust:

Thus says the LORD: "Cursed is the man who trusts in man and makes flesh his strength, whose heart departs from the LORD. For he shall be like a shrub in the desert, and shall not see when good comes, but shall inhabit the parched places in the wilderness, In a salt land which is not inhabited.

"Blessed is the man who trusts in the LORD, and whose hope is the LORD. For he shall be like a tree planted by the waters, which spreads out its roots by the river, and will not fear when heat comes; but its leaf will be green, and will not be anxious in the year of drought, nor will cease from yielding fruit.

"The heart is deceitful above all things, and desperately wicked; who can know it? I, the LORD, search the heart, I test the mind, even to give every man according to his ways, according to the fruit of his doings."

The prophet Jeremiah spoke God's words against the kingdom of Judah, as the Judeans were trusting in human alliances to protect them. They had become like a wilted shrub in the desert; because of misplaced trust, they could produce no fruit. God asks us to withhold putting the kind of trust in people he reserves for himself. According to this passage, if a person puts confidence (meant for God alone) in an individual or group, he or she is "cursed."

This can get tricky, because God uses people and alliances to further his purposes. We aren't to look to these as our source, but only as instruments God uses at that time. People come and go, but our hearts aren't moved, because we're confident in God, not them.

In my SVM2 ministry role, I'm involved in fundraising. A few years ago, I was talking with a group about contributing. They had given in past years, and I was confident they would do so again. Unknowingly, I had slipped into trusting them instead of God as our source. I was stunned when they told me they had decided not to contribute. That morning, before I received word from the group, the Lord highlighted the Jeremiah text above to me. As soon as I got the word about the funds, he brought that Scripture back to mind. I immediately connected the dots and realized I had grieved his heart through misplaced trust. This was an important, though painful, lesson.

Conversely, those fulfilling the lone requirement—trust in the Lord—are "blessed." They make God their confidence; they look beyond human agents. Such believers are like trees planted by water. They receive comfort and enjoyment as they're inwardly secure in God. They do not strive or become gripped by fear when things get tough. Instead, when the heat comes, as it always does, with challenges and obstacles mounting, those trusting the Lord aren't fearful or anxious.

How is this possible? They have been tried over many years, and God has proven faithful time and again. They have not gotten bitter because things didn't go as planned. They have remained tender, eager to please God by keeping their trust centered in him. Doing this over and over produces trust.

Our difficulty in trusting is at the center of our natural, sinful bent. Jeremiah 17:9 reveals that the heart is deceitful above all things; it can't be trusted. Our lack of trust in God regarding circumstances reveals our hearts' depravity. The Lord is jealous for our dependence, as we were created to live this way. Maturing our trust in God is part of becoming saturated with God's presence.

THE MUNDANE

Becoming saturated with God's powerful presence also includes embracing the mundane. Every human being periodically fights the doldrums of a methodical, mundane, uninspired life. This is normal. In fact, most of life is routine and mundane; we all have to pay bills, wash clothes, do dishes, go to work, take out the trash and do other necessary things. In the mundane, God helps us find consistent joy in him, not circumstances. Effective message bearers learn the secret Brother Lawrence did so many years ago as he cultivated the deep presence of God, no matter what daily chores he was involved with.[11]

Human beings often mistakenly look for the next exciting thing to do, thinking we'll find satisfaction and "the will of God" in that thing. We buy the lie that we aren't "in God's will" because life feels mundane. Too many people run from the mundane and run right out of God's will.

3

Embracing Humility

Spiritual Key # 2

A friend of mine was serving in a difficult nation on the Arabian Peninsula. It's a challenge for anyone from a Muslim background to come to faith in Jesus in this country. As a foreigner, this message bearer was treated with a measure of respect and curiosity, and he used this opportunity to speak freely about Jesus. The responses were death threats and threats to the safety of his family. Locals hoped this would provoke fear. Instead, he continued talking with people about their need for Christ—and they were shocked. They knew the threats and asked him why he stayed and continued sharing. He told how Jesus had been a servant to the people, even when they didn't want him, and he was called to the same.

An often-overlooked yet fundamental mark of a thriving message bearer is humility mixed with meekness. Humility isn't merely a virtue God says is a good idea to develop; it's an essence of kingdom life. In one of his parables, Jesus compared the kingdom to a mustard seed. This small seed symbolizes the humility, meekness and simplicity that consistently grow in disciples of Jesus. Humility is the foundation from which a servant spirit matures, and a servant spirit is necessary for a message bearer. We emulate Jesus in the nations as one who came to serve, not to be served (Matthew 20:28).

John the Baptist pointed the way, saying, "He must increase, but I must decrease" (John 3:30). Effectively doing so takes a lifetime of prioritizing the supremacy of Jesus and, conversely, the nothingness of ourselves. Living to increase (or better) ourselves is innate to fallen human nature. The world's systems tempt us to respond with independence from God, which is pride. Giving in to this temptation renders us ineffective in imparting the life of God to those we serve in the nations.

Pride is often a struggle for young disciples with a sense of calling as message bearers. I once served for a short time alongside a young couple straight out of Bible school. They were sharp and gifted, and they had a destiny to serve the nations. All seemed good on paper, but under the surface lurked a growing sense of pride. Through sincere encouragements of recruiters from mission agencies, they had become aware of their giftedness, leadership capacity and natural suitability as message bearers. But the continual affirmations backfired by contributing to pride and an inflated sense of their untested capacities. This manifested shortly after arriving to the field. They proceeded to inform me that our SVM2 ministry strategy was wrong and that I needed to implement their ideas instead. They said that if I would not, they would have to leave our work and serve with someone else. We parted ways shortly after.

THE ROOT OF PRIDE

Pride is a sin the writer of Hebrews was undoubtedly getting at when he taught, "Let us lay aside every weight, and the sin which so easily ensnares us, and let us run with endurance the race that is set before us" (Hebrews 12:1). He's referring to areas of sin common to all humanity and most difficult to get free from. They're easily justified and cause internal upheaval if left unchecked: pride, anger, bitterness, criticism, gossip and the like. If it's possible to put various sins into a hierarchy, pride would be a foundational sin that others spring from. It's a hindrance to progressing in the will of God. It holds believers back, keeping us bound and ineffective for God.

Since the Enlightenment, humanism has been seeping into every segment of society. It's the belief that human beings are inherently good and capable of fixing the world's problems through ingenuity and creativity. It leaves God out of the equation and looks to humanity as the answer. It exalts the creation above the Creator. Humanism is a pinnacle of pride and a mark of the sinful nature standing defiantly in the face of God.

Humanism has also made its way into the church. It tempts believers to serve God out of their natural abilities, education, human sympathies, networking prowess and fundraising skills. The pride of believing we can serve God and his kingdom in our own strength, power and abilities, apart from the leadership of Jesus, reveals our spiritual state.

JESUS' HUMILITY

Humility has been defined as believers' consent to allow God to be all within them, through which they surrender themselves to God's working.[1] This was Jesus through and through in relationship with his Father. He did not rely on his own will (though he was God), but on the will of the Father. The nature of the kingdom of God is self-renunciation and submission to the Father's ways, plans and will. The unyielding self stands in the way of our cultivating humility and obeying the Father. The self justifies its own way, stands up for its rights and seeks its own glory.[2] The power to deny self, allowing the Lord to work brokenness into us, is the life Jesus came to provide. Though fully God and fully man, Jesus voluntarily emptied himself, shining the spotlight on the Father.

We human beings become what we behold. Prayerfully studying Jesus' humility enables message bearers to develop his humility themselves. Gazing long at his humility, specifically displayed through his betrayal and crucifixion, strengthens our capacity to embrace it.[3] Humility is a centerpiece of identifying with Christ among the unreached and unengaged, allowing message bearers to face hostility and rejection without losing heart.

Jesus joyfully laid down his desires as well as his power as God, that the Father might work in him through the Holy Spirit.[4] Every time message bearers respond to Jesus' will over securing status, building reputation or accumulating wealth, God is able to work through us toward ministry transformation.

Jesus' relinquishing of the self life wasn't a burdensome calling. Laying aside rights by submitting to the Father's will produced joy and confidence as peace flooded his soul. It's tempting to think that following Jesus as his message bearer is too hard and that the cost is too high. It's exactly the opposite. Surrendering to Jesus is the on-ramp to joy and exhilaration. Obeying God's ways produces life as it was divinely intended to be lived.

This has helped me in my journey. As a young disciple, I naturally thought I was missing out by inviting Jesus to be Lord through surrendering my own self-importance, a career esteemed by society, the latest gadgets and top-of-the-line clothes. I was being obedient but had no joy in it. But as I meditated on Jesus' humility, I realized I was not losing out but instead was gaining the life I was created for. I try to remind myself of this every time I'm tempted with thoughts of self-pity for what I've "given up" in following Jesus.

"I AM LOWLY . . ."

Jesus taught, "Take My yoke upon you and learn from Me, for I am gentle and lowly in heart, and you will find rest for your souls" (Matthew 11:29). This is one of the few places he described his own character. He could have emphasized his holiness, glory, mercy, power and much more. Instead, he brought attention to his lowliness and gentleness (or meekness). According to Jesus, lowliness is a goal. Becoming a servant of all is our highest priority.

Meekness is power under control—the restraining of oneself for a higher purpose. Opportunities for showing meekness emerge when we are mistreated or in a situation where our perceived rights have been violated. Mistreatment is a tool to test a believer's meekness. Jesus was consistently mistreated yet did not respond. It should not be forgotten, however, that he could have. He had the position and authority (as God in the flesh), yet restrained that power in obedience to the eternal purposes of the Father.

It's the same today. Few will be won to Jesus through a gospel presentation alone. They need a manifestation in the message bearer of humility and meekness, attracting them to the Savior testified about. This is biblical humility and a spiritual key of those serving as Jesus' message bearers. Humility is not natural, which is why when demonstrated it possesses spiritual authority to touch hearts.

WE AREN'T OUR OWN

Paul taught, "You are not your own . . . you were bought at a price" (1 Corinthians 6:19-20). Our human nature tempts us to be self-seeking and self-important. We feel pressure to make ourselves greater in others' eyes, to raise ourselves up, to enrich ourselves and secure ourselves. Self-seeking makes us say anything, do anything and be anything to please another. We resemble the believers surrounding the apostle Paul; he lamented that they "all seek their own, not the things which are of Christ" (Philippians 2:21). Believers easily get sidetracked with the natural priorities of our human nature. We cater to what seems best for preserving self, and we justify our actions accordingly.

This is commonly expressed in making ourselves busy to feel more important. The busier we are, the more we feel needed. Then we elevate this sense of being needed to an unhealthy level. This temptation is common in every culture. As message bearers, we need to fight it as it arises by confessing our shortcomings, humbling ourselves before God.

BEING HUMBLE BEFORE GOD

What does it mean to humble ourselves before God? It means surrendering the self life, which is a concept given much attention in this book. The self life is one reason message bearers aren't seeing more of the power of God working in and through us. God wants to give us so much more, releasing hundredfold blessings through us and our ministries. Yet there is a hindrance. We may have left home, loved ones and jobs in following Jesus, but we haven't necessarily surrendered our old, natural selves.

We're born again, made new creations in Christ. With joy in our hearts, we run the race and fight the battle. Yet it doesn't take long before we face our inability to overcome sin in our own strength. We tell ourselves that if we just try a bit harder, all will be well. We pray—and then sin again. A temptation to question God and to doubt his promises rises. We consider what individual sins we may be guilty of. Instead, the root problem is our nature, which is unclean and set toward its own preservation and ends. What we need is deliverance from that nature.

An important lesson for every message bearer is that, though we may be godly, sincere and earnest, the human nature (or self life) may still be strong within us. The apostle Peter is an example. As he served with Jesus for three years, he healed the sick, cast out demons and preached the kingdom of God. Yet the self life was still operating powerfully within him.[5]

The self life is realized among message bearers through self-comfort, self-consciousness, self-pleasing and self-will. The Lord recently revealed an area of self I had been unaware of. In my ministry, I often relate with non-Western leaders, churches and ministries. When I was asked to speak to a church fellowship made up of Western message bearers in an African nation, I found myself feeling insecure and self-conscious. As I reflected, I realized that we Western message bearers tend to compare ourselves, sizing each other up. We can often feel uncomfortable with each other (much more so if we're from differing organizations). This springs from a self-consciousness that hinders us from rightly serving and loving one another as fellow servants in the body of Christ.

Message bearers genuinely want to get free of the self life, but how? Again, we observe Peter. After his three denials of Jesus, the Lord looked directly at him. That pure and holy look was like a dagger in Peter's heart. The realization of what he had done was driven home with authority. Peter wept bitterly. That night and the following day must have been horrendous for him as he saw Jesus crucified and buried and faced his own betrayal. That humiliating experience was the turning point for Peter, the moment he realized just how powerful the self life was within him—that *he* was capable of such actions. We want to allow the same realization to penetrate our hearts—that *we* are capable of such things. Then turn to Jesus, confessing specific areas of the self life and receive his deliverance by faith.

HUMILITY BREEDS A SERVANT SPIRIT

Humility isn't humanly attainable. It's not natural. But the indwelling Spirit imparts the powerful life of Jesus, enabling us to choose his humility. This surrender isn't a one-time thing but is continually embraced over a lifetime. There will be an initial surrendering to God, breaking the self. God will keep this process current through circumstances, helping us to continue to deny ourselves.

Cultivating humility progresses to developing a servant spirit toward others. Some say it's one thing to submit to God, humbling ourselves before him to rid us of self life, but another thing entirely to do so with others. Our submission to others reveals our level of surrender to God.

While living in Istanbul, Kelly and I had the opportunity to embrace this type of humility. We had been asking God to build our staff team when a couple got ahold of us. They were living in Izmir, Turkey, serving on a church-planting team. The Lord had been leading them to consider another team, as their gifts were more geared toward support ministry. Our work required administrative support, and as we talked, we felt the Lord putting something together.

In the process, they asked if we would be willing to consider moving to Izmir instead of them moving to Istanbul. Kelly and I were surprised, but we told them we would pray about it. As we did, we realized there was nothing tying us to Istanbul, as our work could be done from many locations. More than this, we both felt the Lord asking us to serve this couple by honoring their request. He impressed on us the importance of showing them from the outset that we, as leaders, were willing to make a big change to put their needs before our own.

DENYING SELF

God uses others to help us deny ourselves. This happens through relationships that try us, people who mistreat us and situations we just don't want to be in. Message bearers who have spent a significant amount of time in crosscultural ministry know this is to be expected. In fact, many choose to leave the field because of relationship breakdowns. Have you heard the expression "We can't crucify ourselves"? God uses others and our responses to them to help us deny self.

God is committed to crucifying our natural selves to fill us with the Holy Spirit, making us more like Jesus. The pain we experience because of others should not be wasted in God's kingdom. We can use it to search our hearts for unconfessed pride. Instead of responding negatively to people, we resist pride and embrace Jesus' humility. The degree to which out of our own hurt we respond in anger and bitterness to others (even when justified) is the degree to which pride and self are at work in us.

Jesus' conversation with his disciples the night he was betrayed provides a glimpse of humility producing servanthood: "Jesus, knowing that the Father had given all things into His hands, and that He had come from God and was going to God, rose from supper and laid aside His garments, took a towel and girded himself" (John 13:3-4). Here was the desire of nations, the focal point of history, the one in whom all things consist and exist, the preexistent, eternal God in the flesh, completely aware that God the Father had divested him with all authority, power and eternal reign. He understood the victory to be won through his death and resurrection. His response was to stoop to the lowest level: washing feet. We're meant to live as servants, revealing the true nature of Jesus to others. Loving the body of Christ and putting others before ourselves is part of our calling.

SURRENDERING RIGHTS

Part of human nature is a misplaced belief that we're entitled to various rights. This doesn't disappear when we're born again. We lay down each right as the Lord puts his finger on it, causing an inner shift and an increased desire for God's will. As we do, perceived rights appear smaller over time. Surrendering rights is key to embracing humility. Most would not question that we should renounce things that are wrong. But it gets uncomfortable doing so with things that are legitimate and right.

The world is preoccupied with rights—particularly the Western world, where perceived rights and entitlements are constantly reinforced. Westerners have much to learn from the global body of Christ related to this issue. Examples of rights include "a right to feel superior toward others; what I consider a normal standard of living; the ordinary safeguards of good health; regulate my private affairs as I wish; privacy; my own time; a normal romance if any; a normal home life; living with the people of my choice; running things."[6] God may give these as gifts at various points, but we aren't to presume we're entitled to them.

Several years ago while living in Orlando, Florida, I was considering my rights, a regular practice I had learned years before. I was also praying about buying an investment home in Orlando, as they were so inexpensive. I discerned God speaking to me about surrendering the right of ownership, specifically of a home. It was not a blanket statement saying I should never own a home, but an invitation to lay that "right" down. As I asked the Lord for understanding, he revealed that because of my calling in the global church, he wanted me identifying with leaders who didn't have the same access to resources. To this point I've continued to surrender this right, as my family has thus far only rented homes in the various countries where we've lived.

Jesus provided a blueprint to live the gospel in a self-centered, rights-dominated world. He surrendered the right to a home, a family, marriage, money, consistency and eventually life itself. We partner with him through surrendering perceived rights that define us in our culture but can hinder us as disciples.

IDENTITY IN CHRIST

Message bearers often feel rejected, unloved and unrecognized by others and God. In fact, this is a common state due to our darkened understanding (Ephesians 4:18). Unless we replace these feelings with the truth of identity in Christ, we will have trouble. Human beings naturally seek worth and value in what we accomplish and in how many people recognize us, but these never satisfy the human heart. Deriving value and worth from externals causes unhealthy motivations in our actions and work.

Message bearers easily believe that what we're doing in serving God is of no value. It's insignificant, it isn't affecting anybody, it's a waste of time. We're tempted to quit, and multitudes do, cutting off what might have been. In fact, a temptation to quit is possibly one of the greatest schemes of the enemy among Christians.

God invites us to stop evaluating ourselves using standards other than his. Our self-evaluation expresses itself in a variety of ways, largely depending on our personalities. For some, external measurements like numbers in meetings, converts, Twitter followers, Facebook likes or churches planted in an unreached ethnic group define their identity and value. For others, internal measurements such as perfectionism, self-criticism and busyness do.

The same love the Father has for Jesus, he has for us who have chosen to follow his Son (John 17:20-23). This makes us of eternal value and worth to God, even if we never accomplish anything for him. He wants us to know this truth deep inside, not simply to believe it doctrinally. Developing our identity in Jesus enables us to stop striving to obtain a sense of value and worth through external or internal standards. It frees us to be faithful even when it feels like we're not influencing anyone.

Much burnout in vocational ministry appears to be rooted in misplaced identity. Burnout can be a result of overwork done in the wrong spirit, with the wrong motivation. Working hard is God's will, and we do so from an identity rooted in Jesus, not to gain value from what we do for him. This protects us from unnecessary burnout. I'm aware of this tendency in my life. I'm naturally a hard worker, so I regularly seek to honestly evaluate myself to see if I'm working hard from motives other than the glory of Jesus. Do I derive my value from people's affirmations or from how many people are joining our work or from pleasing those around me or from having a following? If so, I need to realign myself, returning to my identity as one valued by God. This often means taking a day or two from work each month to recalibrate my identity in Jesus.

God is calling message bearers to lay down our desires to be known, to have our own ministries and to receive praise from people. He is calling us to cease striving and manipulating for position and power, to surrender jealousy and envy toward other message bearers. God doesn't freely give his power to those clinging to self-promotion and self-preservation, but to those cultivating humility, meekness and a servant spirit.

THE CAMBRIDGE SEVEN

The Cambridge Seven are an inspiring example to close this chapter.[7] Seven gifted students at Cambridge University in England during the 1880s chose to lay themselves down, answering the call to be God's message bearers to China. Each forsook a promising career. Several were famous athletes known throughout England. Instead of taking the well-worn path of selfish ambition, they denied themselves for the sake of Christ. They did not find their identity in worldly markers others vested in them but in obeying Jesus and following him. Their stunning example was used by God to provoke a generation of new message bearers in the late 1800s.

The body of Christ needs such examples again.

4

Hungering and Thirsting for God

Spiritual Key # 3

Hungering and thirsting for God is essential for message bearers. It grows day by day, rather than being mastered at a certain stage and left behind as we proceed with life and ministry. We often go through seasons; at times we hunger for God and at others we don't. A problem is that some message bearers are in the same place with God today as they were ten years ago. They have failed to move on in hunger and thirst for God.

Here's a common experience: A message bearer has prepared effectively to serve God among an unengaged ethnic group. He is a fervent, spiritually hungry disciple. His spiritual disciplines are well honed. Upon arrival, he seeks God to know what God's ministry strategy is for this people group. In the early days, he seeks God day and night, hungry to know God's heart while developing ongoing intimacy with Jesus. The Lord reveals a plan and strategy that the message bearer implements. In time, the strategy takes shape, work becomes busy, and his spiritual disciplines fall by the wayside. His heart hunger for Jesus slowly dissipates. This continues over a significant period without correction. The message bearer is now a hard worker but has little spiritual influence to give away.

I have friends who have served in Turkey for more than fifteen years. They have been faithful and are extremely hard working. They have bought into the necessity of consistently stoking their hunger and thirst for God. They deliberately organize their schedule to include fasting, prayer, diligent study of the Word and personal retreats with him. Their motivation in these disciplines isn't primarily ministry related. Their purpose is to draw near to the Lord personally to gain spiritual understanding and to produce a growing hunger and thirst. They have faithfully done this for years, in the midst of both good and challenging circumstances.

THE POWER OF THIRSTING

A recurring biblical principle is the correlation between hungering and thirsting for God and obtaining spiritual realities. John tells us,

> On the last day, that great day of the feast, Jesus stood and cried out, saying, "If anyone thirsts, let him come to Me and drink. He who believes in Me, as the Scripture has said, out of his heart will flow rivers of living water." By this He spoke concerning the Spirit, whom those believing in Him would receive; for the Holy Spirit was not yet given, because Jesus was not yet glorified. (John 7:37-39)

Jesus' will is to pour the Spirit on his thirsty children. He loves to quench our thirst, filling and empowering us to do his will among unengaged ethnic groups. We're given three requirements for receiving living water (which is the Holy Spirit). Jesus said meeting those three conditions is essential for receiving the power of the Spirit in life and ministry: (1) possessing thirst for the Spirit, (2) coming to Jesus to receive and drink of him and (3) believing in Jesus according to what the Bible says about him. God is entrusting to disciples that which is of the highest value (the Holy Spirit). Those lacking thirst won't appreciate what they have been given, and God will not give such precious resources to them. Lacking thirst has no bearing on eternal salvation, but it negatively affects our capacity to receive more of the Spirit as his message bearers.[1]

Many hindrances keep us from hungering and thirsting for God. These originate from our self-oriented natures, the world and the enemy. We're consistently bombarded with meaningless substitutes, and we buy into them at various levels. (Social networking, entertainment and the Internet are the most invasive of these today.) It takes a purposeful heart to say no to the substitutes and to position ourselves to desire more of God. Many message bearers have been satisfied with a small measure of what God intends us to enjoy. We've settled for scraps that keep us from partaking of the banquet table of divine resources readily available to us (Psalm 23:5).

Why does God use the imagery of hunger so often in the Bible? Have you seen a person near starvation, desperately doing whatever is necessary to get food? Nothing can distract hungry people from this basic need. They're bent on one thing only. This is the picture of a person spiritually hungry for God. But few are filled spiritually due to a failure to hunger. We subtly believe we can live without more of God. God seeks those who recognize their barrenness apart from the Spirit and cry out to him until he fills them.

ONWARD AND UPWARD IN CHRIST

Developing a hunger and thirst for God means working against our natural tendency to plateau spiritually. Instead of climbing higher in God, we level off. Most often this is unconscious, which is a reason for much of the complacency found in the body of Christ. One of the Spirit's roles is to activate a desire within us to go hard after God each time we level off. He seeks to overcome complacency, to ignite us with renewed hunger and thirst for him. When we position ourselves near the flame of God's love over and over, the Spirit stirs hunger and thirst in us.

In college, I understood it was pointless to hunger for God in my own strength. I visited the tiny prayer chapel on Azusa Pacific's campus early every morning. Mentors had shown me that praying the Bible over my life and using it to worship God would in time create spiritual hunger. And that was my experience as I gave myself to the process of sitting, day by day, near the flame of his love in that little prayer chapel.

Paul began Colossians 1 by giving thanks to God for the faith the Colossians were known for. Then he continued with a prayer for the Colossians to excel in spiritual maturity:

> For this reason we also, since the day we heard it, do not cease to pray for you, and to ask that you may be filled with the knowledge of His will in all wisdom and spiritual understanding; that you may walk worthy of the Lord, fully pleasing Him, being fruitful in every good work and increasing in the knowledge of God; strengthened with all might, according to His glorious power, for all patience and longsuffering with joy; giving thanks to the Father who has qualified us to be partakers of the inheritance of the saints in the light. (Colossians 1:9-12)

This is our consistent aim as well. Too often we rely on victories and spiritual revelations from the past. Complacency begins when we think we've attained a measure of spiritual stature in Jesus and can therefore coast. But God would have us grow daily in spiritual maturity. No matter what heights we reach, there is always much more available in God. He has so many facets to his being. We are finite; he is infinite.

Paul said a characteristic of a Christian life is that it consistently moves on with Jesus. He testified, "I do not count myself to have apprehended; but one thing I do, forgetting those things which are behind and reaching forward to those things which are ahead, I press toward the goal for the prize of the upward call of God in Christ Jesus" (Philippians 3:13-14). Paul was looking forward to greater growth in grace in Christ, and he clearly stated that this lifestyle was the basis for truly following Jesus. To those who think otherwise, he declared, "God will reveal even this to you" (v. 15).

Jesus taught the same principle: "For whoever has, to him more will be given, and he will have abundance; but whoever does not have, even what he has will be taken away from him" (Matthew 13:12). Jesus is saying that those who see and hear will move forward in the things of God. To them, more spiritual understanding and wisdom will be given. Spiritual abundance is given to disciples who are hungry and thirsty for truth, continually seeking God for more. They aren't content with yesterday's spiritual wisdom but instead press on consistently for more. As they set their hearts on grasping the ways of God, in time they receive.

Conversely, those who do not build on their current understanding of the ways of God lose spiritual ground. This is an important caution for message bearers. Serving without spiritual abundance is doing so apart from God's plan. We move upward and onward in Christ by growing in spiritual maturity through receiving greater understanding of his ways. This happens by cultivating spiritual hunger and thirst. Becoming stagnant and failing to grow in spiritual understanding amounts to losing ground and moving backward.

SEEING OURSELVES CORRECTLY

Developing hunger and thirst for God means growing in our understanding of how God sees us, which motivates us to respond with love back to him. God transforms us with the incredible joy he has for us. Why would we love someone who is mad at us or who we can never please, no matter how hard we try? Message bearers often have such misunderstandings about how God views them, which hinder them from hungering and thirsting for him with sincerity.

One reason for these misunderstandings is our thought life. The greatest spiritual battles take place in our minds, in what we say to ourselves. Some refer to this as self-talk, the hundreds of thoughts and inner conversations going through our minds each day. These aren't based in scriptural truth but on falsehoods we pick up from others, our culture and our fallen nature. Here are a few examples: I'm not good enough for God. I can't do what he's asking of me. God could never seriously use me because of my past. Why did God allow this to happen if he loves me? I know God loves me because he has to, but I'm not sure he likes me.

Isaiah 62:4-5 reveals astounding truths about God's thoughts toward us:

> You shall no longer be termed Forsaken, nor shall your land any more be termed Desolate. But you shall be called Hephzibah, and your land Beulah; For the LORD delights in you, and your land shall be married. For as a young man marries a virgin, so shall your sons marry you; and as the bridegroom rejoices over the bride, so shall your God rejoice over you.

The name Hephzibah means "My delight is in her." God says to all who come to him with a sincere heart, though we may be frail, weak and broken, "I delight in you."

Though we may falter and our confidence in God may be weak, he sees our genuine desire to know him and love him. We are often much harder on ourselves than God is. Once we confess mistakes and past sins, choosing to walk obediently in Christ, God remembers our sin no more. He delights in us. He enjoys our small attempts to love him. He isn't disgusted with us because of our shortcomings. He rejoices over us as we fight the battles to keep our hearts fixed on him.

Many message bearers come from difficult family backgrounds. Before coming to Jesus, we may have been involved in lifestyles contrary to God's ways. Jesus has cleansed us, enabling us to live differently, but the memory of our former lives can keep us from moving forward. Our pasts are behind us, but our unrenewed self-talk continues to produce guilt and wrong understandings of God and ourselves. We overcome this self-talk by immersing our minds in what God says and thinks about us. This is what renewing our minds means (Romans 12:2). We replace wrong thoughts with the truth of how God sees and feels about us. I find it helpful to speak these truths out loud. In God's kingdom, there is great power in spoken words. Find verses about who we are in Christ and what he thinks about his people, and speak them.[2]

We love only because God first loved us (1 John 4:19). We love Jesus because of an awareness of his immense desire for each of us, those created in his image, for whom he died. He is turned upside down with joy and gladness when he thinks of us, which he does constantly (Psalm 139:1-6). Message bearers are called to witness to this great love. Wherever we go, we're demonstrations, evidences and proof of that power and love. Succeeding or failing to internalize God's love for us is crucial to our ability to give his love away.

KING DAVID

King David had a hungering lifestyle. A broken man, he was prone to run from God, compromise and blatantly sin, bringing harm to his family and his people. When we look at his life, we can say honestly, "If God can make David into a person after his own heart, there's hope for me!" His secret was that no matter how far he fell, he knew (was assured) God loved him and that he also loved God.[3] Though he was weak and prone to mistakes, David wanted to please God and to bring him glory and honor.

This desire was motivated by a profound hunger and thirst for God that can be traced back to his teenage years. David was a lonely shepherd boy in Bethlehem, worshiping with his harp, pouring out his heart to God. Developing a heart of worship is the beginning of cultivating hunger and thirst for God. We steadily learn to worship and adore him for who he is, what he has done and what his plans and purposes are. In spite of circumstances, we choose to worship rather than complain. Those who pursue a lifestyle of worship in their early teenage years are prepared for great things ahead, though choosing to do it at any age does great good.

We get a glimpse into David's worship encounters by reading the book of Psalms, a profound example of the wholehearted worship God intends for his people. Throughout the psalms, we catch a view of the range of emotions inherent in the worship process. We vicariously enter David's exuberant highs and devastating lows. The book of Psalms is a powerful school for every message bearer to study and apply as we develop hunger and thirst for God. I find it helpful to read the psalms aloud, using them as a springboard for my own worship and adoration of God. An example is Psalm 18:1-3:

> I will love You, O Lord, my strength.
> The Lord is my rock and my fortress and my deliverer;
> My God, my strength, in whom I will trust;
> My shield and the horn of my salvation, my stronghold.
> I will call upon the Lord, who is worthy to be praised;
> So shall I be saved from my enemies.

THE ROLE OF ADVERSITY

An important skill to develop for thriving as message bearers is seeing God in the midst of adversity. Responding correctly to adversity propels us into hunger and thirst for God. We read in Acts 14:21-22, "When they had preached the gospel to that city and made many disciples, they returned to Lystra, Iconium, and Antioch, strengthening the souls of the disciples, exhorting them to continue in the faith and saying, 'We must through many tribulations enter the kingdom of God!'"

It's easy to forget that the body of Christ was never meant to be a majority. We enter the kingdom through a narrow gate. Throughout its history, whenever the church became popular, it failed to be the salt and light it was called to be. It watered down its message and ceased to live on the cutting edge. When Christ's body functions as she ought, tribulation, pressure and opposition are the norm.

Due to the human propensity to avoid pain, believers often fail to endure hardships, adversities and challenges. If responded to correctly, troubles will always produce purer faith in Jesus. We want to be able to tell stories of faithfulness in testing, yet we often aren't willing to go through the test. We want to get out of painful circumstances as soon as possible. In doing so, we sometimes unknowingly cut off the very thing God intended to use to shape us and bring spiritual expansion.

Because of its ability to get our attention, God often uses pain to teach us. This is why Paul could honestly say, "I am filled with comfort. I am exceedingly joyful in all our tribulation" (2 Corinthians 7:4). On the surface, we wonder what Paul was thinking. As we peel away the truth of God's use of adversity, we begin to see it as a gateway to hungering and thirsting for God. God's promises of enabling grace are reserved for those facing hardship. Those in persecution bear witness to this, and many are surprised at the nearness of God in the midst of great trouble.

Proverbs 24:10 says, "If you faint in the day of adversity, your strength is small." In the same vein, God said to Jeremiah, "If you have run with the footmen, and they have wearied you, then how can you contend with horses?" (Jeremiah 12:5). How can we be trustworthy in all God wants to do through us if we can't overcome the annoyances and adversity we face today? God matures us by walking with us through hindrances. This training is a lifelong process. As we overcome, God orchestrates new challenges that take us to new levels of faith.

Kelly and I experienced a season of adversity surrounding finances when living in Izmir, Turkey. The Lord used several forms of guidance to prepare us. One morning, the Holy Spirit highlighted Psalm 66:10-12 to me, which speaks of God testing his people, refining them. I knew something challenging was coming. Verse 12 culminates the section, promising that God will bring his people out to rich fulfillment.

Two nights later, Kelly had a vivid dream. Our family was in her childhood home. A large tornado was coming straight for it. We ran to the basement while the tornado blew over the house. Upon inspection, the tornado had damaged only a small portion of the living-room roof. And everyone was fine.

The next day, I read in a book that faith is the ability to trust the complete wisdom of a holy God, who can't do anything wrong. Though challenging circumstances arise, as they did for Jesus, will we implicitly trust the character of the Father, who can do nothing wrong?

We sensed God speaking to us through those three forms of guidance, though we were unaware what they referred to. About a week later, we got an email that our financial support account showed a large deficit. It surprised us but didn't faze us, as the Holy Spirit had prepared us beforehand for this "tornado."

God knew this challenge was coming and prepared our hearts to respond in faith instead of fear and worry. This produced great joy as God showed us there's nothing we experience that's outside his loving gaze. God had led us into the trial to refine and purify us. The promise of Psalm 66:12 is that God brings us out with abundant fulfillment, and he did this over the coming months as he faithfully supplied our need. Seeing the ways of God in action coupled with his kind guidance in preparing us elicited one response: growing adoration and worship for this God we love and serve.

Some think we "graduate" from obstacles as we develop spiritual maturity. In fact, it's the opposite. The challenges get bigger and more involved as God requires greater dependence on him at each new step. This is a common point of trouble. Instead of looking to God in the current situation, we look back and do what worked in our previous experiences. Moses did this when he struck the rock for water instead of speaking to it (Numbers 20:7-13). He presumptuously thought the answer to the current problem was the same as the previous time. God was teaching him not to rely on a ritual or formula but only on him.

5

Being Clothed with God's Word

Spiritual Key # 4

Today believers tend to lack biblical knowledge and understanding. Though it's difficult to prove, some say this is the most biblically illiterate generation of the modern age. It appears believers aren't interested in the hard work of being consistently spiritually taught by God through proactive study of and meditation on the Bible.

Several years ago, I worked with a short-term mission team made up of disciples preparing to serve long term among an unreached ethnic group. They were asked to write testimonies using Scripture to show unbelievers what it meant to be spiritually lost. What Scriptures would they use to show what God has done for humanity through sending his Son? Very few knew what Scriptures to use.

In contrast, a Ghanaian message bearer serving in North Africa has the essential spiritual key of being clothed with God's Word. When he and his wife first arrived in Mauritania, God led them to focus on intercession for the first several years of their ministry. During that time, the husband went deep into prayerful study of the Bible, memorizing entire books. However, it was more than mere mental memorization, as God's truth marked and changed him. When he speaks, he strings Scripture together, interweaving Old and

New Testament passages. He knows them so well, it appears they are his own words. His entire messages simply link Scriptures together on a given topic. He rarely deviates to add his own stories or illustrations, as he believes Scripture itself has the best ones. He simply lets the Bible speak for itself. And his teaching has spiritual authority that deeply impacts multitudes.

One of the evil one's tactics is to keep message bearers powerless. He has no trouble defeating message bearers who know the Bible only in a cursory manner. His strategy is easy to identify but difficult to fight amid the current cultural malaise. The body of Christ needs to push beyond the low status quo of cultural Christianity. We need to align ourselves with God's standard for his people, as those meditating on Scripture and becoming fascinated with Jesus. I'm not referring to memorizing Scripture apart from it being alive within us, apart from it impacting our lives as it's applied. I'm also not referring to a mere intellectual exercise of "knowing" Scripture. We want spiritual understanding so we discern the heart and ways of God and have our own hearts stirred with love as we draw nearer to him.

Overall, the church has succumbed to a low standard for equipping Christ's body with spiritual understanding of Scripture, as we expect so little of God's people. How can we expect to be faithful as God's message bearers apart from God's Word dwelling in us, set ablaze by the Spirit?

CLOTHED WITH GOD'S WORD

What does it mean to be a message bearer clothed with God's Word? Bobby Clinton, one of my professors, defines what he calls a Bible-centered leader, and here I apply his definition to the spiritual key of message bearers being clothed with God's Word: their life and ministry is informed by the Bible; they have been shaped personally by biblical values; they have grasped the intent of scriptural books and their content and can apply them to current ministry situations; and they use the Bible in ministry to impact others.[1]

Alternatives to being clothed with God's Word include being fad centered—reading the Bible somewhat, but being more interested in the latest spiritual fad than the Scriptures themselves; being tradition centered—reading the Bible somewhat, but being more influenced and molded spiritually by what is expected from a particular group, denomination or organization; or floundering—reading the Bible somewhat, but being at a loss as to how to encourage others and speak into their lives using God's Word.[2]

EZRA—CLOTHED WITH GOD'S WORD

Ezra was a priest and scribe after Israel's seventy-year exile in Babylon. He helped rebuild the spiritual condition of the Israelites inhabiting Jerusalem after their captivity. The Israelites did not have regular access to God's Word during the exile, making Ezra's ministry of the Word all the more important. Ezra 7:10 tells us, "For Ezra had prepared his heart to seek the Law of the Lord, and to do it, and to teach statutes and ordinances in Israel." He knew how to use God's Word in varying situations. He had a reservoir of biblical understanding, experience and spiritual knowledge because he was a devoted student of God's Word. God used him mightily to revive the spiritual life among the Israelites, and the key was that Ezra himself had first been changed by spiritual truth.

We prepare ourselves for ongoing ministry, as Ezra did, by diligently filling the reservoir of spiritual truth within. As we minister to others, God brings stored truth to the front of our minds. If we don't have truth alive on the inside due to a failure to study and apply God's Word, he can't bring it to mind.

Ezra not only studied God's Word but also set his heart to do it. The blessing is in the *doing* of the Word, not in the studying alone. Ezra wasn't content with mere intellectual exercise; he understood he needed to do something with the truth he grasped. He responded to study with action. Few have seen the dynamic impact of the Word of God as Ezra did. Are we willing to pay the price Ezra paid to have the spiritual authority he walked in?

During college, I worked for a season as a janitor at a church in Pasadena, California. Cleaning the sanctuary and offices became my prayer closet, as the mindless work lent itself to wonderful interactions with God. One day, the Lord spoke clearly to my heart, asking, "Are you willing to pay the price?" I knew he was referring to being clothed with his Word. I surrendered to the Lord, replying that no matter what it took, by his grace, I would pay the price to walk in his presence, clothed with the Word of God. I made up my mind on that day to become an Ezra in my generation.

THE RIGHT APPROACH

Believers know God calls us to his Word. We often hear we're supposed to be reading our Bible and having a "quiet time." This can leave us feeling guilty if we don't live up to a certain expectation. We want to get away from the sense of duty (and guilt) this puts on us and instead embrace the privilege of fellowshiping with God through studying, meditating, praying and applying his Word.

As a young believer, I did not enjoy reading the Bible. Those in spiritual leadership encouraged me to do so, and so I did. But I did it merely out of duty. I loved God and wanted to serve him, but I could not understand the Bible and what God was trying to teach through it. Over time, as I stuck with it, the Spirit slowly helped me understand and gave me a passion for the Word that has not abated. I was recently teaching a Bible series on Colossians in our equipping school in Chiang Mai. An Indonesian brother commented, "You have such deep insight in the Word. You are hungry to find every nugget of spiritual truth from every verse and apply it to our lives." I assured him I did not start that way.

When we approach the Bible from a religious perspective, it's dull and unattractive. We experience it in a whole new light when we come to it, saying, "Jesus, I want to know you in every way possible. I want to understand your ways and your thoughts. I want to burn with love for you, your church and the lost, and I want you to teach me divine mysteries." This prayer has become the consistent cry of my heart since my early twenties.

As a message bearer, it's tempting to think that if I'm not directly involved in a ministry of speaking to groups, I do not need to be clothed with God's Word. No matter the type of ministry we are in—working with orphans, church planting, business as mission, teaching English, teaching literacy, outreach to prostitutes, inner-city work or whatever—we need to be continually clothed with God's Word.

Through the Word, God reveals Jesus and his ways, gives us daily direction, feeds us spiritual meat, builds our inner beings and gives spiritual perspective and understanding. How few believers truly appreciate the privilege of accessing the great Author of the universe through his Word? Every class of human being—rich and poor, educated and ignorant, young and old—is welcomed into the King's chambers through his Word. The greatest experiential knowledge of God and his ways is available equally to all—on one condition: that we search his Word, pray it daily, obey what we've gleaned and make it our own.[3]

JESUS AND THE WORD

Why has God made his Word such a priority? Our foundation in Jesus is laid through trusting him for salvation. What is the process of building on that foundation? We hear and do the Word of God (Matthew 7:24-27). Or, put another way, we diligently study and apply God's truths to our lives. Through the study and application of God's Word, message bearers are built into the people God ordained us to be. Apart from this, we find it impossible to do the will of the Father among the nations.

The Bible is called the Word of God, and the same title is given to Jesus (Revelation 19:13). The Bible and Jesus have the same essence and nature—both are the Word of God. Each is the perfect revelation of God, completely agreeing with the other. The Bible thoroughly reveals Jesus, and Jesus perfectly fulfills the Bible. The Bible is the written Word of God, and Jesus is the personal Word of God. The Spirit perfectly reveals God through his written Word and through the Word made flesh—Jesus himself.

THE DISTINGUISHING CHARACTERISTIC

A proof of being a follower of Jesus is devotion to God's Word. Jesus gives the benchmark of a disciple: "If anyone loves Me, he will keep My word; and My Father will love him, and We will come to him and make Our home with him" (John 14:23). Four important points are found in his statement: (1) keeping (or obeying) God's Word is the biggest factor in being called a disciple; (2) keeping God's Word is the greatest test of our love for God; (3) Jesus manifests himself to the disciple through his Word as it's kept; and (4) the Father and Son abide with the disciple through God's Word.

The distinguishing characteristic of Jesus' followers is keeping (or obeying) God's Word. Salvation is more than believing right doctrines. It is having heart belief and building a life committed to obeying God according to his Word. As God's message bearers, we teach unreached ethnic groups this distinguishing characteristic by consistently modeling a lifestyle of one clothed with and obeying God's Word.

A pastor in Thailand recently told me the Evangelical Fellowship of Thailand (EFT) conducted a national study to discover how much Bible reading Thai believers were doing on a regular basis. The results surprised many leaders in the Thai church. The study concluded believers were reading on average a few verses a week. The same scenario could be repeated in many countries. This has led me to believe that a truly necessary ministry at present is in-depth Bible teaching that ignites believers through personal study and application of the Word.

MAKING TRUTH OUR OWN

John 13:17 is an often-overlooked verse carrying an important truth for message bearers. Jesus had just washed his disciples' feet and told his disciples why. He then made this statement: "If you know these things, blessed are you if you do them." Jesus distinguished between *knowing* the truth and *doing* it. Many churchgoers know intellectually about Jesus yet haven't laid their lives before him as Lord. Likewise, message bearers often have not applied biblical truths, though we "know" them to be true doctrinally.

Listening to biblically solid, anointed messages isn't the same as applying the truths listened to. To carry spiritual authority, message bearers need to experience truth. James tells us, "Be doers of the word, and not hearers only, deceiving yourselves" (1:22). One believer gets excited about a particular truth but isn't changed by it. Another is stirred by the Spirit, determining to make truth her own by *doing*. As we *do* the Word, it becomes our own. In acting on truth, we receive God's blessing.

How does God help us make truth our own? First, we encounter a specific truth while reading the Bible, hearing a message, observing something in nature, watching a movie, reading a book or in some other way. The truth makes us pause, and we may even be in awe, but that doesn't mean it has become real in us. Next the Lord presses us with our need for that truth, and this is often where we miss it. It is common to think that because we've heard a certain truth many times before, it has become real in us. We must interact with that particular truth through experience. God wants it to be real to us.

This is the process of writing truth on our "inward parts" (Psalm 51:6).

Why is this important for God's message bearers? Spiritual equipping on crosscultural ministry means a growing measure of truth written on our inward parts through experience. Without truth written within us, we have only dry, religious words to offer those we serve.

Be aware that communication gifts do not give us spiritual authority. Authority comes as God takes us deep into a living understanding and application of his Word through our obedience. The church I grew up in in the jungles of Papua New Guinea is now in its third generation of believers. Begun in vibrancy through powerful encounters revealing Jesus as superior to the spirits, the church has become nominal. I recently asked my dad (the original message bearer among the tribe) what he thought had happened. He lamented, "The pastors are giving messages they have been taught to give by others but which they don't really understand." In essence, they aren't living the truth of the messages and therefore lack spiritual authority in their communication to others.

The angel told the apostle John, "Take and eat it," referring to the scroll (Revelation 10:9). John was to ingest the spiritual truths the scroll taught, making them his own, allowing them to teach him through experiential knowledge. Then he was to proclaim those truths to others. When we "eat the scroll," we're marked by what it communicates. It becomes a part of us at the core of our being. Only after eating could John rightly communicate all God intended to teach through the book of Revelation.

One of my greatest joys is learning from brothers and sisters from many nations and cultures who are clothed with the Word of God. I receive a rich deposit as I dialogue with them about Scripture and how eating it has transformed them. My theology and my perspective on the Bible have been enriched as I've gleaned insight through cultural lenses different from my own.

TAUGHT BY THE LORD

The Lord is seeking to teach message bearers *himself*. As David prayed, "I have not departed from Your judgments, for You Yourself have taught me" (Psalm 119:102). This is our vision—to be disciples the Father himself instructs.

Many of us have learned from Bible teachers, commentators, pastors, mentors, missionaries, small group leaders and so on, and this is good and right. There is eternal value in commentators and teachers, as the Holy Spirit works through the corporate wisdom of the church, not just through individual teaching and study. Then we take what we receive from others and bring it to the feet of Jesus, inviting him to teach us himself. Through the consistent work of becoming devoted students of God's Word, welcoming the Spirit to guide us, he teaches us. He uses spiritual teaching from many sources (nature, books, conversations, commentaries, teachers, blogs, podcasts and more) to mature us as we yield to him.

While living in Turkey, I had many opportunities to learn from the Lord, as I did not have the consistent diet of spiritual teaching I'd previously enjoyed. This is common for message bearers among the unreached and unengaged. I directly sought God to teach and mold me. He taught me through various spiritual books and through studies of specific Bible books. Yet I learned to focus my growth on Jesus, not on what a commentary or book said. I valued the different ideas conveyed, and as I meditated, the Spirit gave me a clearer understanding related to Scripture and how to apply it.

This was especially true as I studied the book of Acts and the seven churches in Revelation 1–3, much of which took place in modern western Turkey. These accounts became more real as I was living in the very places they had actually happened. I grasped insights I would otherwise not have understood. Through visiting a variety of ruins connected to biblical times, I was able to put myself in those circumstances.

Some of the most spiritually mature disciples I know did not have regular Bible teaching after coming to faith in Christ. This is often the case for those coming to Jesus among unreached ethnic groups where hostility is present. They submit to the Spirit to lead them and plunge into prayerful study of Scripture. The Lord himself is their teacher, providing light concerning truth and what it means in their circumstances. In time, they're exposed to the important community aspects of teaching, but their foundation in being taught by the Lord was already firm. Such disciples appear to possess inner strength and courage other believers often lack.

A THREE-FOLD PRESCRIPTION FOR BLESSING

The Bible advocates a three-fold prescription for blessing and biblical prosperity and a life pleasing to God. First, let's consider Joshua as God spoke to him about the crucial importance of meditating on the Word.

"Only be strong and very courageous, that you may observe to do according to all the law which Moses My servant commanded you; do not turn from it to the right hand or to the left, that you may prosper wherever you go. This Book of the Law shall not depart out of your mouth, but you shall meditate in it day and night, that you may observe to do according to all that is written in it. For then you will make your way prosperous, and then you will have good success." (Joshua 1:7-8)

Faithfully meditating on, studying and praying Scripture is more than a good spiritual discipline. It's the primary means for message bearers to receive spiritual strength and courage in the face of challenges. It releases divine enabling to walk in obedience. Courage and strength to obey God is imparted as a disciple goes deep into God's Word.

One morning, a verse came with authority during my Bible reading:

Let the righteous strike me;
It shall be a kindness.
And let him rebuke me;
It shall be as excellent oil;
Let my head not refuse it. (Psalm 141:5)

I also read a similar verse in Proverbs that same morning. The Lord impressed on me that something was coming that would be hard to hear yet was meant to serve my ongoing development in humility and meekness. That morning I had a meeting with some British friends from the local Thai church we're involved with. They informed Kelly and me that we had made some cultural mistakes that had offended some Thai believers. We were tempted to defend ourselves, but I was reminded of God's Word that morning and knew God was teaching us not to refuse correction. We were strengthened to respond rightly by just listening and taking in what they had to say. Courage was imparted to humble ourselves as we obeyed God's Word.

Written about five hundred years after God's word to Joshua, Psalm 1:2-3 challenges us to buy into a lifestyle of meditating on Scripture as the pathway to prosperity in the things of God: "But his delight is in the law of the LORD, and in His law he meditates day and night. He shall be like a tree planted by the rivers of water, that brings forth its fruit in its season, whose leaf also shall not wither; and whatever he does shall prosper." Much spiritual meat is packed into these two little verses. Those with a heart to serve God should study all of Psalm 1 in depth, as this chapter captures the heart of a message bearer clothed with God's Word. Five essential qualities are revealed in it: stability, consistency, endurance, integrity and perspective. Do we need and want these in our lives and ministries? Cultivating a lifestyle as a student of God's Word is the way to obtain them. There are no shortcuts.

Many years ago, I made a covenant with God that I wanted to be the man in Psalm 1. I understood that to succeed I needed a lifetime perspective on developing in the Word of God. Part of my commitment was not to waste days, weeks, months, years and even decades that could be used in diligent study, prayer and application of God's divine truth. A practical outworking was the development of a personal Bible-study plan (see "A Bible Study Action Plan" ahead). I've seen a measure of the five essential qualities noted in Psalm 1 taking root in my life as a result of committing to be an in-depth student of the Word of God.

About one thousand years after God's words to the psalmist, the Holy Spirit repeats himself a third time in unmistakable terms. This time it's in the New Testament, which allows no one to claim that blessing through devoting oneself to God's Word is an old-covenant promise. James stated, "He who looks into the perfect law of liberty and continues in it, and is not a forgetful hearer but a doer of the work, this one will be blessed in all he does" (James 1:25). Focused and deliberate study, meditation, prayer and reflection on Scripture provide a message bearer true spiritual blessing and influence.

The Word of God is a book of law, a river of life and a mirror reflecting the deepest parts of our beings. It's meant to convey God's will, impart God's life and unveil God's transforming power in all circumstances. A message bearer who neglects consistent study, praying the Word and diligent application makes a fatal mistake. The greatest secret of growing faithfully in grace, godliness and spiritual influence is abiding in God's Word—using it to search our hearts, turning it into prayer, persistently aligning our lives with it and teaching it to others.

CROWDED OUT

Many message bearers are grateful for the Word's inspired wisdom and life-transforming power. It has set us free from countless areas of bondage and waywardness. If you ask us if we spend time regularly studying the Word, we sincerely respond, "Yes!" Yet when we analyze our schedules, we often realize we haven't spent as much time as we thought.

Also, for many message bearers Bible study is haphazard. We open the Bible to whatever place it falls and read a few chapters. Later in the week, we go to a Bible study and read a few chapters related to that study. Two days later, we read a devotional that takes us to a different book of the Bible, and we read a few chapters from there. We get some of the Word in us, but in a random sort of way. This doesn't allow us to get a firm grasp of its meaning and spiritual implications.

Message bearers who seek to be effective need a focused Bible study plan. Due to busyness, we need to deliberately plan for meditating on the Word or it usually will not happen. We may need to cut excesses (entertainment, time with others and so on) from our lives to pursue in-depth Bible study. This type of study brings joy and excitement as we engage with God's eternal Word and grow our spiritual capacities.

A BIBLE STUDY ACTION PLAN

Developing as students of God's Word takes time.[4] Just as when we exercise a muscle that we haven't used recently, there can be an initial discomfort with Bible study. For in-depth Bible study to become a normal, everyday practice, we need to make a steadfast commitment and ask the Spirit to empower us to become fervent students of the Word. We seek him for divine illumination producing spiritual understanding, not just grasping with our natural minds.

As a young disciple, I was exposed to a number of approaches to Bible study, as many of us are. Most didn't stick, due to my lack of diligence as much as anything else. After much trial and error with various models, I settled on the following approach. I've been following this model faithfully for over a decade, and it has revolutionized my approach to God's Word.

Begin by prayerfully choosing specific Bible books to study over a given year. Which books are you naturally drawn to? Which books do you find most exciting and appealing? Which has God used to develop you in the past? You might lean toward a certain scriptural focus based on your calling, personality and spiritual wiring. You might choose to study only one book or maybe three or four. Some people like to develop an annual plan that includes at least one book from each of the various portions of the Bible, which provides a good grasp of the full revelation of Scripture. This means studying a book from the Pentateuch (Genesis–Deuteronomy), from the historical writings (Psalms, Proverbs, Esther, Ecclesiastes, Daniel, Chronicles, Ruth and Song of Solomon), from the Prophets (Joshua, Judges, Samuel, Kings, Ezra, Nehemiah, Job, Isaiah, Jeremiah, Lamentations, Ezekiel and the twelve minor prophets), from the Gospels and from the Epistles.

I find it helpful to devote myself to studying one book or topic at a time. This provides focus as I grasp the entire purpose and theme of that particular book, getting a bird's-eye view. No book in the Bible is wasted or unnecessary. It has been added to the canon by the Holy Spirit to communicate a particular message not communicated as clearly through any other book.

Writing down the name of the books you plan to study in depth will help you stay focused. While working through a book-by-book study over a year, you might be tempted to focus on a book not on your list. Be flexible as the Holy Spirit leads, but remain focused. The list will help you be diligent.

Besides the books you plan to study in-depth, simultaneously read the Bible devotionally. One pattern used effectively is to read a couple of psalms, one proverb and a chapter or two in a Gospel each day. Reading psalms enables consistent adoration and praise. Proverbs help cultivate spiritual wisdom, understanding and knowledge. And the Gospels allow us to be taught by Jesus himself (the Word in flesh and the foundation of all teaching).

A helpful model for in-depth study is to first read the whole Bible book, without trying to grasp all the spiritual principles and insights. Try to read it in one sitting. This gives you the basic story line and will likely open your eyes to things you miss when you read the book in chunks. Sometimes I read a book fifteen to twenty times through before starting in-depth study. As you read, ask the Holy Spirit to reveal truth to you throughout. Ask him for spiritual wisdom, revelation and understanding related to the book and to the individual chapters. It's good to allow the Spirit to teach us various principles before looking at what others have to say about the text.

To begin your second step of in-depth study, make sure you have access to a notebook (or laptop or tablet) and at least two commentaries (many online commentaries are available). Then begin a portion-by-portion study, using commentaries to observe how different people divide the book and its chapters. Often they break down verses into groupings of four to ten.

Use the commentaries to get historical input and other background information about a specific passage. Write down the verses you are studying (for example, Colossians 1:1-4) along with the gist of what is taking place in them. Then write down spiritual principles you have drawn from those verses. Write down specific applications for God's people. Consider the ways of God and principles of discipleship being alluded to. Consider promises in the text; jot these down and apply them to your life as a prayer. Consider ideas and interpretations the commentaries provide. Write down your thoughts and insights.

If we begin to study the Bible in depth regularly in our twenties, we develop a storehouse of spiritual insight by the time we're forty or fifty. In my twenties, I set a goal to study half the books of the Bible in this way by the time I was forty. At thirty-nine, I'm closing in on that goal.

Faithfully keeping a study notebook on book-by-book studies provides many teaching insights God can use to serve those you minister to. I've studied many books of the Bible, plus various topics and pivotal passages, using this model. It has invigorated me spiritually as I've gone deep with God in his Word, while simultaneously enabling me to prepare messages, series and various talks based on studying and meditating on God's Word.

6

Discerning God's Guidance and Revelation

Spiritual Key # 5

While living in Turkey several years ago, God began to lead Kelly and me toward a relocation. It unfolded over time, starting with a dream. Through the dream, the Lord reminded me of a crucial part of my calling. Over the previous decade, God had put it in our hearts to see a training center raised up to serve the Great Commission. We had thought it might happen in Turkey, but we recognized that wasn't God's will for that season.

Over the next few days after the dream, I asked the Lord if there was another location. As I waited on him, the city name Chiang Mai in Thailand was pressed on my mind with tremendous spiritual authority. I knew this wasn't my own thought, as I knew very little about Chiang Mai and had never been there. I even had to look it up on a map.

When I approached Kelly with the idea of a relocation, she excitedly told me the Lord had been speaking to her about such a move too. Now I was beginning to get excited. I wondered, *God led both of us independently to the idea of a move; will he also put the same city in our hearts?* I asked Kelly if God had spoken to her about a specific place. She said, "Just this morning, God highlighted

Chiang Mai to me!" We were ecstatic. How cool is God?! Of course, this gave us confidence in his will. And we proceeded to ask him to confirm the leading we were sensing.

Soon afterward, we sent a prayer alert to our personal intercessors, inviting them to pray with us about a relocation to Chiang Mai. A seasoned intercessor friend asked if I had read the book *Abandoned to God,* a biography of Oswald Chambers, the author of the popular devotional *My Utmost for His Highest.* She and her husband had just read it and thought it might have ideas for the school we were considering. She had no idea that in 2006 I had read that biography, and God had used it to first envision me for our eventual training school. I had written down several key principles Chambers had used, even detailing ways to set up such a school. God used this connection to confirm he indeed was in this unfolding process.

Two months later, I was in Bucharest, Romania, speaking at meetings. I told a friend that we were praying about a relocation, and out of the blue he said, "Chiang Mai is a key mission hub city. You should consider moving there." Another brother who knew nothing about how God was leading us mentioned he had been praying for us, and God had given him an impression (or picture) in his mind's eye. He saw the city of Istanbul and a huge red arrow pointing east, with the word "east" in large letters. He asked if this meant anything to us.

God had given initial guidance, then confirmed it, yet we wanted even more clarity. We wanted to know why he was leading us away from Turkey to Thailand. We were aware he was doing something but wanted to understand more of what was behind this major move. Over a few weeks, God highlighted eight specific, practical reasons the move was his plan. After arriving in Thailand and getting settled in during our first six months, we could already see the wisdom of God related to the eight specific areas he gave us.

Our hearts were overwhelmed that God, in his goodness, had guided us into a situation that would perfectly meet the needs of our work for the coming season.

RECEIVING REVELATION

We can hear the voice of God! This truth is crucial for fruitfulness as God's message bearers. Revelation is God's self-disclosure to his people. It's his initiative in revealing truths that believers otherwise would not know.[1] God provides two specific types of revelation: general and specific. *General revelation* refers to God revealing himself through nature and through an internal witness within every human being. General revelation isn't enough for developing a relationship with God; it points the way toward him. There is need for more revelation if a person is to develop a relationship with God through Jesus. This is *specific revelation* revealed to us through the Bible, the person of Christ and the ministry of the Holy Spirit.[2]

Receiving revelation begins with believing God is worthy of trust and wants to communicate with us. Communication includes accurately sending and receiving information. We're usually quite good at the sending piece; we know generally how to make our needs known to God. But receiving information from him is a little more uncomfortable.[3] God has provided the communication resources we need to rightly relate with him. Yet many believers in general and message bearers specifically don't know how to hear from God in daily life and ministry.

Without God's guidance and revelation, we do not know where to go, what to do or how to do it. The work of the Great Commission is Jesus.[4] As partakers in this grand calling (Colossians 1:12), we attune our spiritual ears to what he's saying.

Guidance and revelation are based on relationship, and Jesus values relationship above all else. This is one reason he doesn't lay out formulas for hearing his voice. He seeks an intimate relationship of growing understanding. Of course, there are clear scriptural principles concerning hearing God's voice, yet these are applied in the context of a living and vibrant relationship with Jesus.

THE FOUNDATION

Jeremiah 33:3 presents a foundation for rightly relating with God. God says through the prophet Jeremiah, "Call to Me, and I will answer you, and show you great and mighty things, which you do not know." An alternate translation for the word *mighty* is "inaccessible." The Greek word refers to hidden truth. Some interpret this as God having certain truths he doesn't intend people to know, but this doesn't fit the character of the God of the Bible. Instead, only those possessing the Spirit and deliberately seeking understanding accurately grasp the meaning. Hidden, or inaccessible, truths are God's way of beckoning us to wholeheartedly seek him for understanding. When we come across Scriptures that elude us, we need to set our hearts to call on Jesus to reveal the hidden truth.

James 4:2 reveals a significant spiritual principle: "You do not have because you do not ask." This is simple, yet often overlooked, and it's a reason we often don't hear God's voice. Message bearers who persistently ask, seek and knock are given spiritual understanding over time. We follow the example of the widow, who came before the judge day by day until he finally gave in (Luke 18:2-5). God doesn't need to be convinced to "give in," but he wants genuine desire and persistence in obtaining leading, guidance and spiritual truth.

THE SPIRIT OF WISDOM AND REVELATION

Paul understood the need for ongoing spiritual understanding and revelation in the lives of believers. We do well to pray his power-packed apostolic prayer daily—both for ourselves as well as those we serve:

> That the God of our Lord Jesus Christ, the Father of glory, may give to you the spirit of wisdom and revelation in the knowledge of Him, the eyes of your understanding being enlightened; that you may know what is the hope of His calling, what are the riches of the glory of His inheritance in the saints, and what is the exceeding greatness of His power toward us who believe, according to the working of His mighty power. (Ephesians 1:17-19)

This prayer highlights resources needed to hear the voice of God. We receive revelation from Jesus through growing in fellowship with him. The Father gives understanding by providing the "spirit of wisdom and revelation in the knowledge of him." The "spirit of wisdom and revelation" is the indispensable piece of discerning deeper levels of spiritual understanding.

The term *wisdom* used here is the same one used in the book of Proverbs. Proverbs consistently exhorts believers to seek wisdom, understanding and knowledge. To seek is to ask God to open treasures of spiritual wisdom, understanding and knowledge of his truth, ways and will. God is longing to unlock the Scriptures for persistent believers. We can look at the same verse over and over, discerning a new nugget of insight each time.

As we ask the Lord to unveil spiritual wisdom and revelation, he does so in increasing measure throughout our lifetime. I got ahold of this in my midtwenties. During a particular season, I was spending much devotional time in Proverbs. I saw the necessity of asking God to reveal truth from his Word and help me understand how to apply it. I was stirred to consistently pray, "Lord, teach me spiritual wisdom, understanding and knowledge that I can't know apart from your revelation." I expected God to answer immediately, but I've learned that he does this over time as I continue to seek him for it. As I look back over fifteen years of praying this prayer, I see that he unveiled deep understanding as I sought it from him.

KNOWING OUR CALLING

In Jesus' kingdom, every believer has a general calling: loving God with all our heart, mind, soul and strength; bringing as much glory and honor to Jesus as possible; surrendering to the Spirit's discipline of conforming us to the likeness of Jesus; impacting society with the power of the cross and resurrection of Christ. In addition, we need to know the specific realm of ministry God has ordained us to walk in. This is especially true for message bearers.

Paul said he was appointed "by the will of God" (Colossians 1:1). This distinguished him from those who promoted themselves to spiritual authority through striving, manipulation or fleshly ambition—in essence, by their own will. Like Paul, we have the resources to discern the will of God for ministry. This discerning primarily happens as we grow in "the spirit of wisdom and revelation in the knowledge of him" and as we ask him to show great and mighty things related to our purpose. Jesus wants us to have the inner confidence of living in the center of God's purpose as we're put in circumstances, positions and roles by his hand. He wants us to be firm in knowing he has placed and positioned us "by his will." Lacking spiritual confidence of our calling opens us to second-guessing and other attacks.

While I was living in Los Angeles many years ago, the Spirit began stirring in me a vision of my involvement in mobilizing the body of Christ toward the fulfillment of the Great Commission. One day I went with a friend to visit a friend of his. They spent time catching up, and we prepared to leave. But then she prayed for us, and when praying for me, she asked for things in line with what God had been putting in my heart. She asked that the whole world would open before me and that message bearers would be mobilized to the hardest places of the world. I had never met this woman, and she had no idea what was stirring in my heart. Of course, this increased my confidence that God was truly leading me into such work.

When I was twenty-three, during a morning of sweet fellowship with Jesus, I heard him say, "When you are twenty-six, you will begin your life's work." It came with authority, but I was thoroughly disheartened because it seemed so far away. I acknowledged it, submitting to his wisdom. Over the next years, I faithfully did my work, and I forgot about that guidance. When I was twenty-eight, the Lord reminded me, and I saw how he had faithfully brought his words to pass. Near the end of my twenty-sixth year I had begun a global research project looking at trends surrounding Great Commission mobilization across the body of Christ. That project led directly to the launch of Student Volunteer Movement 2 in the following year. That year-specific guidance God provided and fulfilled boosted my confidence that I was walking in the center of his will.

BIBLICAL PRINCIPLES

Many biblical principles help us discern God's voice and receive revelation from him. These help prevent us from making mistakes as we grow in hearing the voice of God.

- We believe that God speaks and that we can hear him (Colossians 1:9).

- The purpose of all guidance and revelation is to know Christ more intimately.

- The Holy Spirit is God's representative, and he gives revelation (John 16:13).

- The Bible is the final authority regarding all guidance and revelation (2 Peter 1:19-20).

- Guidance and revelation are always accompanied by God's peace.

- Direction from God needs to be responded to with action and obedience (James 2:17).

- Divine revelation comes as we cooperate with God's standards and requirements (Isaiah 58:10-11).

- Having revelation and guidance doesn't mean we know the future.

- God's guidance and revelation aren't always easy to hear.

- Receiving God's guidance and revelation is a skill to be developed (Luke 11:1).[5]

Our capacity to hear from God is strengthened through applying these principles over years and decades.

All message bearers need ongoing leading and clarity from the Lord. Yet, as we mature in hearing God's voice and responding in obedience, it seems the Spirit lessens the degree to which he speaks. As we grow in faithfulness and sensitivity, we develop a spiritual reservoir that helps us discern the Lord's guidance without specific direction from him. As we mature, we grow with the mind of the Lord. We possess a growing measure of his wisdom, and the Lord expects us to function according to what he has taught us. No longer does every decision require specific guidance.[6]

It's this way with children. Parents very deliberately teach everything to their small children. As those children grow, the parents don't need to teach in as much detail. They expect their children to act on what they have been taught, and the children know what is expected of them. The Lord is no different, and we are his children.

In my late teens and throughout my twenties, the Lord spoke to me in some astounding ways. The specificity of his guidance was surprising. Much of it has come to pass, while much is still ahead. As the years have passed, he continues to speak, but not with the same clarity and frequency as before. This is one reason I journal what God speaks to my heart and through others. I can reread what God said years and even decades ago and discern the timing of its application.

SOME OF THE WAYS GOD SPEAKS

God speaks to his people in multitudes of ways, and it's good to learn about them in order to build a sense of expectation in us. What are some of the ways he speaks?

- He speaks as we meditate on the Bible. Often a verse jumps out and penetrates our hearts. The Holy Spirit clarifies something specific to our hearts. This is the inner leading of the Spirit.

- The still, small voice of the Lord is probably the most common form God uses to speak, outside of the Bible. As we quiet our hearts, waiting for him to speak, he often moves us in a faint but unmistakable way. When this happens, I've learned to ask, "God, is that you speaking, or is it my own thinking?" If it's him, the sense will grow, not diminish.

- Another common form is impressions. These are pictures in the mind's eye, or a Scripture reference or words that come to mind.

- God can speak through circumstances. We need to be careful, however, not to jump to a conclusion based on circumstances alone, as many factors can be involved.

- God speaks as we live in spiritual community, such as through mentors, counselors and friends.

- God gives visions in our hearts or as if on a movie screen. They often are filled with symbolism related to something the Lord is saying.

- God speaks through dreams. Most dreams are random accumulations of our activities. However, at times the Lord speaks in and through dreams. We need the Holy Spirit's sensitivity to distinguish the difference.

- God speaks through angelic visitations and his audible voice. These aren't as common as other forms, yet they still take place.

- At times the Lord speaks to other people on our behalf (often referred to as personal prophecy). Through one of the above means of guidance an individual is given a direct revelation about something the Lord wants to communicate. Often the person speaking will not understand the meaning, but it makes complete sense to us.

- God can speak through nature, movies, news and any other media. He isn't limited in the means he uses. The key is learning to discern his still, small voice and know when he's speaking and when it's our own thoughts, others' ideas or the enemy's suggestions.

Ways God Speaks

"For God does speak—now one way, now another—
though no one perceives it." (Job 33:14 NIV)

Ah-ha experiences	Depression (negative)
Angelic visitation	Discerning of truth
Animals/birds	Discontent that leads to godly clarity
Anointing presence	
Art—observation of others' works	Discussion with others
Art—process of doing	Dreams
Audible voice	Dynamic reflection
Bringing things to remembrance	Events
Check in your spirit, warning, red flag	Feeling held by presence/love of God
Circumstances	Feelings
Classes/seminars (e.g., seminary, training center, college, conferences)	Grief
	Gut-wrenching knowledge
	Hunches ("holy hunches")
Confirmation through others	Ideas
Creation and nature	Imagination

Incense—fragrance of God

Inner sense

Intuitive sense of God's presence coming on you

Inward witness of the Holy Spirit

Journaling

Joy, sometimes sudden

Know that you know

Literary means (e.g., Christian writers, devotional books, poetry, novels)

Ministry to others

Music—secular and sacred

Opening the Bible and finding the passage speaks to you or your situation

Others speak God's word to you

Parables or analogies from life

Peace or lack of peace

Pictures (may or may not be connected with Scripture)

Preparation for teaching/preaching

Prophecy

Quickening word, phrase, passage or reference from Bible

Quickening of heart through sight, sound, smell

Restlessness or unsettled feelings

Relationship with children

Retrospect

Revelation

Secular movies, plays, events, etc.

Silence

Something "jumps out at you"

Speaks to you through your own words (as you are speaking)

Speaks to you through others' words (unconsciously or unplanned)

Still small voice (not necessarily audible)

Stringing Scriptures together

Talking to God

Thoughts (may or may not be connected with Scripture)

Trances (e.g., John in Revelation)

Trials and suffering

Visions

Weeping, rush of weeping in presence of God

Woken by God in the middle of the night

Worship

Written word—quickening a verse or passage (in or out of context)

Written word—seeing truth, instruction (in context)

By Elizabeth Glanville (unpublished paper, begun 1994); used by permission.

HEARING AND SPEAKING GOD'S WORDS

The importance of the gifts of the Spirit is becoming more apparent to message bearers. That's partly because of the confusion and pressure around us in global ministry. We need as much spiritual wisdom, understanding and knowledge as possible to accomplish God's purposes.

Spiritual gifts need to be demystified. No stream, denomination or movement owns the gifts of the Spirit. They aren't just for super saints but for all disciples from every background. They are for all calling on the name of Christ. God's spiritual gifts are tools for edifying Christ's body and fulfilling the Great Commission. Neglecting them is refusing resources God has provided to accomplish his plans.

A primary gift the Lord has provided for the Great Commission is prophecy.[7] Paul taught, "Pursue love, and desire spiritual gifts, but especially that you may prophesy" (1 Corinthians 14:1). This implies that all believers have the capacity (at varying levels) to prophesy, because all believers have the ability to hear God's voice (John 10:3-4). To prophesy is simply to fellowship with Jesus, discern revelation of his ways, heart, plans and purposes, and communicate that revelation to others.

Paul reveals an important principle when he calls believers to pursue prophecy above the other gifts of the Spirit. As we live in intimate fellowship with Jesus, we hear God's voice more clearly, and the other gifts of the Spirit are activated. When the Lord gives divine information or we receive impressions from the Spirit, the groundwork for the other gifts is simultaneously laid. The gifts flow from consistent fellowship with Jesus as we seek his wisdom and spiritually discern his heart. This is why Paul exhorts us to desire prophecy.

When I was twenty-five and serving in my church's college ministry, I thought my future ministry might involve using the local church in the United States as a platform to help college students develop a heart for the Great Commission. During that year the Lord used a sixty-day period to speak to me about widening my vision. He used two lay leaders in my church and one leader from North Carolina to expand my vision. After I preached one night in our college ministry, a lay leader came to me and declared rather abruptly, "Ryan, your vision is too small. Raise your sights. Raise your vision!" Three weeks later, in a mentoring group with the pastor, another lay leader pulled me aside and said, "God is going to use you in ways beyond your ability to comprehend now. What you've been dreaming of is too small!" About a month following this, my pastor was on a call with a pastor from North Carolina. During the conversation, that pastor sensed the Lord giving him specific prophecies for people in our church. He asked if there was someone named Ryan working with the college ministry. Our pastor said yes. The other pastor said to tell me, "God is going to use you wonderfully. There is a strong call on your life."

WAITING FOR THE FULFILLMENT

There is one principle of guidance that, if overlooked, can trip us up: the importance of timing. We often assume that the thing the Lord reveals will come to pass immediately. But usually it's a picture of something Jesus wants to bring down the road—sometimes years or even decades later. Much spiritual preparation, uprooting, cultivating of disciplines and faithful waiting are usually required to be mature enough to handle what God intends to bring. And usually the greater and more widespread the potential impact of a ministry, the longer the wait until the fulfillment of the guidance.

Sometimes we judge what we hear from God as invalid if it doesn't come to pass in our time frame. But he's unveiling a vision of something that will be, but at the moment is not. So we need to align our hearts with his and ask him to bring the thing to pass according to his will and timing. In the meantime, God causes the seed of the guidance to germinate and grow. Usually this takes place without us or others noticing. We continue praying and waiting in faith, yet nothing seems to be happening. Then suddenly, when it has reached maturity and we are prepared, God brings the vision to pass.

Some mistakenly assume a revelation will come to pass no matter what we do in the meantime. This isn't a correct understanding of prophecy. We cooperate with God's purpose in the meantime, trusting God to bring about the actualization of the guidance in his timing. We keep watering the seed of the vision and weeding the soil of our hearts of anything entangling us. We resist discouragement and actively wait for the fulfillment, keeping our hearts free of unbelief. We don't dictate to God the "how" of bringing the thing to pass. And we contend in prayer for the thing the Lord has put in our heart.

The biblical norm is that much time stands between God's revelation of a vision and its fulfillment. Joseph waited twenty-two years from having the dreams of his brothers bowing down to him and the fulfillment of those dreams. David waited close to twenty years from being anointed king by Samuel to receiving the crown. God wants us aware of his timing so we don't get discouraged and quit.

This has been a great encouragement to me. As mentioned, in my early to mid-twenties, the Lord gave me glimpses of what he wanted to do in me and through me during my lifetime. If I had not known the importance of God's timing and actively waiting, I would certainly have gotten impatient and off track. Along the way, the primary point God instills is the importance of vibrant relationship with him.

7

Pursuing a Lifestyle of Prayer

Spiritual Key # 6

The fulfillment of the Great Commission can be actualized as each disciple takes responsibility for it. As message bearers, a primary piece of our calling is intercessory prayer, because we impact our work and our geographic area through it. Yet just as important is communion prayer, which fuels our lives in God. As we cultivate a heart of prayer for the nations, we encounter deeper intimacy with God.

The spiritual key of prayer has been divided into two parts in this chapter, because intercessory and communion prayer are two sides of the same reality.

Communion prayer focuses on God for who he is. We talk to him about our desire to grow in him and to have our hearts expanded. We meditate on his attributes, characteristics, work and ways, responding with adoration and worship. Apart from regularly abiding and fellowshiping with the Lord in this type of intimate prayer, we can't know what we should intercede for. So failure to operate in communion prayer hinders a message bearer's fruitfulness for God's kingdom.[1]

Friends of mine provide international leadership for a large mission agency. They have extremely busy lives with travel, meetings and other responsibilities. Yet they're committed first to communion prayer. It would be easy for them to allow pressures to drive them instead of being driven by their life in God. This couple commits to regular prayer walks in nature, setting aside portions of their day just for communing with Jesus, and they have periodic fasts when they get away with God. Their intimate fellowship with Jesus enables them to face the challenges of their role with spiritual clarity and power.

Joshua experienced this abiding fellowship with God when he joined Moses on the mountain, where Moses privately met with God for forty days and nights. This left Joshua, Moses' aide at the time, the same length of time to meet with God by himself (Exodus 24:13). God was developing in young Joshua a deep hunger for his presence that would mark him throughout his life.[2] Joshua went into the tent of meeting and remained there (Exodus 33:11), developing a love for God's intimate presence.

A deep love for the presence of God is foundational for effectively serving him. In my midtwenties, I had a special place to be alone with God. In the middle of Pasadena is a beautifully landscaped campus with streams, gardens and benches. Four to eight hours a week, I walked that campus or sat on a bench, where I dialogued with God. I took my Bible, my journal and a book along. In this natural, quiet environment I had some of my most memorable interactions with him. It became such a special place that I proposed to Kelly there.

BEING WITH US

We find Jesus' desire to live in intimate fellowship with his children in Mark 3:14-15: "He appointed twelve, that they might be with Him and that He might send them out to preach, and to have power to heal sicknesses and to cast out demons." Before sending his disciples out to preach, heal and deliver people from demons, he wanted simply to be with them. Such being together was the foundation of the subsequent release of spiritual power to go about "doing good and healing all who were oppressed by the devil" (Acts 10:38), just as Jesus had done by his own example.

Jesus loves being with us. Do you believe that? He desires to be with you more than anything or anyone else. If you have received Jesus' work through the cross and resurrection, you are his treasured possession, the apple of his eye, his favorite one. Because he is God, he can have billions of favorite ones. I once heard someone say this, and I dismissed it. Then I began praying it over my life, and it changed my outlook. I truly am God's favorite, not in comparison with anyone else, but because I possess intrinsic value as one who chooses and obeys his Son.

We exist to enjoy deep relationship with Jesus. This is his primary will for us. Communion prayer releases confidence (spiritual strength), which is the basis of intercessory prayer. Because they had "been with Jesus," Peter and John could walk in boldness before the Jews (Acts 4:13). We can't confidently intercede according to God's will, rightly discerning and praying his heart, without abiding in intimate fellowship with Jesus. We pursue this life in secret, in the "secret place" (Matthew 6:6). We do not enjoy communion with Jesus primarily through public meetings, though we do not neglect those. We hide away in secret, gazing at the whole spectrum of God revealed in Jesus.

Some assume time isn't important in relationship with God. They cite God's unchanging love and acceptance when arguing that the amount of time spent in prayer doesn't matter. It's true that God's love and acceptance aren't affected by how much time we spend with him. However, our ability to fellowship and abide with him is. Sensitivity to his voice and the ability to be moved by his heart and to discern his leading take place as we know him more and more.

Communion prayer takes deliberate effort and sacrifice to maintain. There is a cost. We need a measure of abandonment to walk in it. We choose to dispel distractions to set ourselves toward this end. Many things arise to keep message bearers from growing in intimate fellowship with God. Pressures, needs, deadlines, friends and so on will come to the forefront when we commit to going deep with God.

A few generations ago, E. M. Bounds, a great teacher on prayer, declared,

> We need a generation of preachers [message bearers] who seek God and seek him early. Who give the freshness and dew of effort to God and secure in return the freshness and fullness of his power that he may be as the dew to them, full of gladness and strength, through all the heat and labor of the day. Our laziness after God is our crying sin. The children of this world are wiser then we. They are at it early and late. We do not seek God with ardor and diligence. No man gets God who does not follow hard after him.[3]

FOLLOWING OTHERS

As stated, we learn from observing the spiritual disciplines of others. It's not hard to see a connection between their prayer lives and the fruitfulness of their ministries.

- Charles Simeon (Anglican pastor in England in the 1700s) spent every morning from four until eight with God.[4]

- John Wesley spent two hours a day in prayer.[5]

- Robert Murray M'Cheyne,[6] a Scottish preacher in the late 1800s, stated, "I ought to spend the best hours in communion with God.

It is my noblest and most fruitful employment. It is not to be thrust into a corner. The morning hours, from six to eight, are the most uninterrupted and should be thus employed."[7]

- Adoniram Judson, the first American message bearer, sent in 1812, commented, "Arrange your affairs, if possible, so that you can leisurely devote two or three hours every day not merely to devotional exercises but to the very act of personal prayer and communion with God."[8]

Martin Luther's famous quote makes this point: "If I fail to spend two hours a day in prayer each morning, the devil gets the victory throughout the day." He also lived by the motto "He that has prayed well has studied well." Luther understood the dynamic connection between intimate fellowship with Jesus and discerning Scripture and its practical application to our lives. Those fellowshiping with Jesus understand and correctly apply the mysteries of God's Word and speak relevant words to others.[9]

In our day, communion prayer is difficult due to the technology all around us. Between the incessant pull to check Facebook, post a witty tweet, respond to an important email or read a text, we're never really alone. I find it helpful to set boundaries related to media. The early morning hours are my time to fellowship with God, so I try not to open email, get online or respond to any texts or Skype calls before eight in the morning. Periodically, I take a media fast, pulling away from my phone and online connections for a day or two to quiet my heart before God.

COMMUNION PRAYER IMPACTS CHARACTER

Communion prayer is a means of cultivating a character like Jesus'. Lasting character transformation comes as we receive more of his life. Areas of life not yet under his leadership begin to change. Developing character is a natural by-product of engaging with Jesus with an honest and open heart. This is a requirement for being spiritually equipped as God's message bearer.

Our speech is crucial in thriving as God's message bearers. One reason some disciples aren't producing more fruit is a failure to be careful in speech. This is a consistent challenge for me. Almost twenty years ago, I heard a penetrating message about guarding our tongues. In response, I wrote on a three-by-five card, "May this be my personal bond—speak evil of nobody." I signed and dated it, and then taped it to the inside cover of my Bible. Whenever I'm tempted to criticize people, I glance at the card. I don't want my kids being raised hearing Kelly and me talking negatively about people. Unfortunately, I've failed countless times. Yet it's a value I continually pursue.

Jesus provided a high standard concerning words when he said, "For every idle word men may speak, they will give account of it in the day of judgment. For by your words you will be justified, and by your words you will be condemned" (Matthew 12:36-37). Words encouraging devotion, perseverance and spiritual strength in others will be rewarded. Criticizing and discouraging words will be judged, and the believer will suffer regret before the throne of God (apart from repentance and turning from such words). This doesn't refer to eternal condemnation (if a born-again believer) but a penetrating awareness before God that we grieved his heart.

It often appears that message bearers aren't taking this teaching seriously. Many of us verbalize misgivings about people, churches and ministries. We complain flippantly about petty issues instead of possessing a thankful heart. We criticize others when they do things in a different way than we may do. Our words are often motivated by subtle yet deeply rooted pride we aren't aware of.

Another way to develop Christlike character is in relationships. Relationships among believers are under attack on all sides, and breakdowns among Christian leaders, friends and coworkers happen often. When we lack commitment to authentic relationships and to dealing rightly with people, it's difficult to thrive as God's message bearers. Demonstrating authentic love is a testimony among the lost, but it also empowers us to withstand assaults on our relationships.

One reason for many relational breakdowns is that we have been hurt. Painful words were spoken. Events cut to the core of our being. How we respond each time we're hurt reveals our level of meekness and character. I love talking with older believers whose spiritual lives are vibrant and free. They have had myriads of opportunities during their lifetime to get bitter due to mistreatment. But with every circumstance, they chose forgiveness and blessing.

Leaders in ministry are often misunderstood. Once I wrote to a leader of a major mission association, asking for advice on a proposed ministry project. He wrote back with a scathing response, accusing me of motivations I didn't have. Pride and defensiveness arose within me, but the Holy Spirit checked me. I discerned immediately that this was a test to see how I would respond to mistreatment. I calmed myself, took a day and composed a gentle message that spoke directly but not emotionally to his false accusations. He sent a message back apologizing for being quick to accuse without having the correct information.

WHY PRAYER WITH FASTING?

A key to our calling as message bearers is developing an environment, through communion prayer and fasting, where God can present himself among an unreached people group with great authority. Throughout the Bible as well as church and mission history, we observe men and women with lives of prayer that few attain. Many coupled their prayer lives with fasting.[10] In the Old Testament, fasting was often a sign of turning from sin. In the New Testament, it unleashed spiritual power, bringing victory and maturing God's people spiritually. Fasting has been called the atomic power of the prayer life.[11] It's a spiritual tool that is being reawakened and joined with committed and faithful prayer.

Fasting plays a role in pulling down spiritual walls among the most unreached ethnic groups and raising laborers of high spiritual quality among them. Many hindrances will not be overcome except through lifestyles combining prayer with fasting (Matthew 17:21). A lifestyle of fasting involves periodic longer fasts (from solid food) as well as regular daylong fasts or abstaining from periodic meals.

Fasting enlarges our hearts as we behold Jesus. Our hearts grow in desire for him and become more sensitive to his leading. Our capacity to receive spiritual insight increases, and we gain spiritual understanding from the Spirit. Our minds become illumined with the spirit of wisdom and revelation (Ephesians 1:17) and sharpened with understanding and insight into the Word. Fasting therefore helps develop decision-making ability according to God's will. It also solidifies our identity as sons and daughters of God, and the distractions of the world grow dimmer.[12]

Kelly and I, with our SVM2 staff, facilitators and alliance ministries internationally, undertake a three-day fast every three months while observing weekly fasts on Tuesdays, affectionately called SVM2uesdays. Throughout the year, we're sensitive to the Spirit as he leads us to additional longer fasts.

We do not rely on fasting itself but on God's ability to use this means of grace to produce heightened sensitivity within us. If we evaluated fasting based on one or two occasions, we might conclude it isn't effective. However, after cultivating a lifestyle of fasting for more than a decade, we attest to the amazing power of fasting to bring change. Much guidance from the Lord has been the product of our hearts being prepared through fasting. It's possible we would not be serving as we are apart from fasting's spiritual benefits.

In 2011 we relocated our SVM2 international office to Chiang Mai. We needed a suitable place to host our soon-to-be-launched

Mobilizer Equipping Schools. We found a facility close to our office that appeared ideal, but we encountered many difficulties as we negotiated with the owner. We felt led to do a three-day fast with our staff to see if God had anything to show us about how to proceed. On the last day of the fast, a member of the staff had a friend tell her of another place in the city for rent. It had been used previously as a small international church. We met the owner, looked it over and sensed the peace of God. It was perfect for our needs, complete with a library/study room and an already outfitted prayer room. We quickly signed a contract, and the building has been a wonderful environment for training non-Western leaders.

REASONS FASTING IS EFFECTIVE

Why does God care about a lifestyle characterized by prayer and fasting? He loves when we're motivated by his love to practice discipline. When we master our appetites (emotional, physical, relational), his heart is moved. Fasting has nothing to do with earning God's love; nothing we do qualifies us to be accepted by him. Yet God is pleased when we humble ourselves, choosing to lay our appetites aside to be further changed into his likeness. We don't fast to get from God; we fast to become more aligned with him. Fasting helps rid us of the clutter of life.

Fasting prepares us to fellowship with God in a greater capacity. When we fast, he enables us to hear him more clearly, to sense the movements of his heart more dramatically. We understand Scripture better, and we more easily empty ourselves of the self life and enter into God's presence. Sometimes these happen during the fast itself and sometimes down the road. As a result, we want to make fasting a lifestyle choice, not merely a one-time event.

Fasting is a voluntary, loving response of obedience. It is never to become an empty ritual done from religious obligation, as it was for the Pharisees in Jesus' day.

FASTING, REPENTANCE AND THE GREAT COMMISSION

The prophet Joel saw far into the future to a day when the Spirit would be poured out. This prophetic promise was given after the people responded to God's mandate in Joel 2:12-17. It is important to see the process here. The Israelite leaders were to call a gathering in sacred assemblies across the land, so the people would turn to him with all their hearts in fasting and repentance. This call was to take the highest priority, even before being married (v. 16). No one was exempt, as even babies were to come. After this widespread event, God promised an outpouring of the Spirit (Joel 2:28-32). We find a divine pattern here: repentance and fasting are precursors to God unleashing his power in the earth.

There are important implications here for message bearers. In Joel 2:32, we observe God's purpose behind the Spirit's outpouring: a global harvest of unbelievers brought into the kingdom by the millions. This is what we contend for in the nations. In the book of Joel, believers en masse genuinely confessed, turned from sin and walked in God's standards, which was directly connected to an increasing spiritual harvest among the nations.

God has a divine pattern to produce global harvest now and in the future: Fasting and prayer align our hearts with God, provoking repentance, and in turn repentance moves God's heart to release mercy on the nations. We see the same pattern in 2 Chronicles 7:14: "If My people who are called by My name will humble themselves, and pray and seek My face, and turn from their wicked ways, then I will hear from heaven, and will forgive their sin and heal their land."

At the initial outpouring of the Spirit during Pentecost, a measure of the promises prophesied in Joel came to pass. Peter stood up and declared that Joel had spoken of this phenomenon (Acts 2:14-24). This was a direct reference to the ushering in of the new "gospel" age, enabled and empowered by the Holy Spirit. The prophecy in Joel has continued to come to pass in various measures throughout history as God's people have followed the divine pattern of fasting, repentance and prayer. It will culminate in an unprecedented harvest among all ethnic groups prior to the events surrounding Christ's second coming. The fulfillment of the Great Commission will be preceded by mass numbers of disciples around the world coupling their prayer lives with the discipline of repentance and fasting. These disciplines will be followed, in God's timing, by a global harvest motivated by the Holy Spirit.

We're contending for revival that will draw millions to lasting, transformative faith in Christ.[13] An often repeated prayer in my heart is "Lord of the Harvest, raise up 100,000 new high-quality message bearers to reap a global harvest of 100 million souls from among the unreached/unengaged." Psalm 118:16 declares that the "right hand of the LORD does valiantly." When God moves in this way, light is shed upon hearts, providing the understanding that God isn't merely another god or religion, but the essence, source and originator of all things and the final word.

A literal fear of God settles over people when Jesus is seen as high and exalted, creator, sustainer and initiator of all human life. Conviction of wrongdoing is rampant, as grief and mourning clings to people. The Word of God is spoken with authority, hitting people where they are, moving them to respond from the heart. Signs and wonders reveal Jesus' government over the physical realm. They testify that Jesus is alive, breaking defenses as people see him to be real—though many continue to harden their hearts.

In 2006, God gave me a small glimpse of the influence of repentance and spiritual awakening on mission. I was speaking that January during Asbury College's annual Great Commission Congress in Wilmore, Kentucky. Though I was to speak on issues related to crosscultural mission, the Lord led me instead to talk about the correlation between spiritual awakenings and the mobilization of Christ's body for the Great Commission. I called the students to abandoned devotion to Jesus, to following him according to his standards of discipleship. At the close of the last chapel service, I invited the student body to kneel and repent of sin they had been tolerating in their lives. The presence of God was tangible in the room.

Two weeks later, I received an email from Asbury's spiritual life director that an awakening had broken out on campus. That Monday, after chapel, the worship team had kept playing as many students worshiped and repented. Many wept openly before the Lord as conviction struck their hearts. The college canceled classes, as students stayed in the chapel building day and night until the next week.

Several months later, I was told a large number of students from Asbury had signed the "GO Declaration," a commitment to go to the unreached as God's message bearers after graduation. What had happened? The students' repentance and encounters with God had prepared the way for their hearts to respond to God's gentle provoking to serve him among the unreached.

INTERCESSORY PRAYER

Intercessory prayer is Jesus' chosen way to release heaven's resources on the earth.[14] It's his primary means of moving his eternal plans and purposes forward. Many words have been used historically to refer to this type of prayer, including *victorious, persevering* and *prevailing*. Modern terms include "strategic intercession" and "kingdom prayer." Intercessory prayer is prayer on behalf of people, families, cities, nations and situations; we stand in their place, contending for the will of God, transformation, conviction of sin and the influence of the kingdom among them. There is a law in the kingdom of God that this type of intercession, committed to faithfully, produces results. We don't know how long it may take, but if we stick with it, aligning with God's conditions of intercession, he will not fail to act.

Intercessory prayer is the most important of ministries, yet generally the least utilized. As message bearers, our prayer lives are part of our work. This is so basic, it hardly needs stating, yet it's so easily overlooked. The work of message bearers is spiritual, and intercessory prayer is central to producing spiritual fruit.

Prayer and intercession are part of our job, not something to do when we have spare time. But prayer is almost offensive to our minds. Human nature wants to *do* something. Intercession seems like a waste of valuable time compared to what could be produced through action. The Lord sees it differently. He values the "foolishness" of disciples praying and not leaning on their abilities and capacities alone. Prayer reveals our poverty of spirit. Jesus commends this as the first beatitude in his Sermon on the Mount (Matthew 5–7). Being "poor in spirit" means recognizing our need for God in everything. This is the beginning of true intercession.

Some of our friends work in a difficult country in the horn of East Africa. They worked hard as message bearers for twenty years with little observable fruit to show for it. Around the twenty-year mark, the Lord led them to recruit a team member who would do nothing but pray. This woman was incredibly faithful in doing the hard work of focused intercessory prayer daily. During the following year, breakthroughs started happening. Their work began producing fruit, and openness to the gospel, which they had not experienced before, began marking the local people. They knew something spiritually shifted when the woman joined them to pray.

A large, global evangelistic ministry doing widespread literature distribution implemented a twenty-four-hour prayer room at their headquarters. This prayer room has been staffed day and night by people praying for the work of this ministry around the globe. The organization has seen a significant increase in the numbers receiving Christ and being baptized and in the number of churches planted globally. They're the first to tell you it's the committed, intense intercessory prayer for souls in the prayer room that changed the situation on the ground.

THE INNER WORKING OF PRAYER

It's easy to misunderstand prayer. Many of us think if we bother God long enough, he will answer. We get into crisis situations and pray with zeal for the circumstance to get righted. Our prayer is shrouded in worry, anxiety and turmoil. But effective prayer emerges from a grateful heart at peace and quiet before God, even though we may find ourselves in a swirl of challenging and emotional circumstances. Prayer requires a heart waiting on the Lord in the place of rest. Learning to live perpetually before him in stillness is needed to operate according to God's ways of prayer and intercession. This contrasts with the inner upheaval, worry and turmoil often experienced in our prayer lives.

Prayer, in its simplest form, is a cycle. Through the Spirit we discover what God wants in a given situation, and we intercede for his revealed will to be accomplished. We pray what is on his heart, and in response, God works according to his perfect will.

God could take our little piece out of the prayer cycle and be just fine. But because of his eternal plan to partner with his people in bringing his kingdom, he involves our small efforts and uses them for his glory. Could failure to see God's intended will taking place be due to self-centered praying instead of praying the discerned will of God? Or could it be because we resist the Spirit's zeal for transformation around the world? Many give up on prayer because of what they see as inconsistency on God's part. Instead, we have not aligned with God's prerequisites, so we haven't seen the results we know God's Word promises.

Answers to prayer are the real test of intercessory prayer. Andrew Murray, a South African pastor and author during the late 1800s, once said, "This is the fixed eternal law of the kingdom, that, if you ask and receive not, it must be there is something amiss or wanting in your prayer. If no answer comes we aren't to sit down in sloth that calls itself resignation, and suppose it is not God's will to give an answer. No, there is something in the prayer that is not as God would have it, childlike and believing!"[15]

THE SPIRIT OF PRAYER

There are two graces of intercessory prayer. The first is a general grace God gives to intercede. This is general help in prayer as well as a daily enabling to make time for it. We are generally unaware of this grace taking place. We often don't feel much inspiration, and it is work to remain faithful to prayer. Yet if the grace to do it were removed, we would fail to pray in even the smallest way.

The second is a unique grace given by God at specific moments in which he grips us. At such times, the Spirit labors through us in intercession. Zechariah 12:10 reveals this unique grace: "And I will pour on the house of David and on the inhabitants of Jerusalem the Spirit of grace and supplication." The word *supplication* can be interchanged with *prayer*.

At certain times, God releases special grace to individual disciples, adding to their general prayer and intercession and taking them to a new level of spiritual authority. Paul wrote about the Spirit's involvement in this: "Likewise the Spirit also helps in our weaknesses. For we do not know what we should pray for as we ought, but the Spirit Himself makes intercession for us with groanings which cannot be uttered" (Romans 8:26). Such intercession often feels like a great weight or burden. No one can work this up or make it happen; it isn't based in emotions. We cooperate with it by giving ourselves faithfully to individual and corporate intercession as often as possible. This allows God the opportunity to grip us in this unique way. And it almost always results in spiritual power being released, convincing unbelievers of the terrible wrath to come outside of Jesus. Most of the significant awakenings of the past three hundred years were preceded by this kind of intercession.

The Moravian movement of the mid-1700s teaches much about

this important subject. The Moravians motivate us to hunger and thirst for a higher, deeper level of intercession. In the 1720s, Count Ludwig Von Zinzendorf welcomed a community of persecuted Christian refugees to live on his estate in Moravia (modern-day Germany). Over time, this community grew into a thriving revival center. John Wesley visited the Moravians many times for spiritual refreshment, citing rich encounters with God each time.[16]

Zinzendorf was a deeply spiritual man of prayer. In the communities' early days, there had been divisions among the refugees. He asked God to bind hearts together in love, and God answered with a revival in 1727 of such quality that relationships were immediately mended. Conviction of sin was rampant and heavy. The revival's power was sustained for years, as these believers would not speak negatively against one another.[17]

After the initial phase of the revival passed, the community set up a round-the-clock prayer watch, seeking God for depth of spirituality and growing interest in crosscultural mission. The emphasis was shaped by a commitment to send message bearers marked with spiritual authority. God gave them a deep burden through intercession marked by anguish and a heightened intensity for souls.[18] They sought God to release conviction on people, remove spiritual blinders and enlighten hearts to recognize their deep need for him.

The Moravian prayer watch became the fuel for their crosscultural ministry and lasted unbroken, around the clock for one hundred years. Known historically as the "100 Year Prayer Meeting," it facilitated prayer and intercession that sustained the ongoing sending and fruitfulness of large numbers of message bearers. The percentage within the Moravian community of those sent as message bearers is the highest any church or denomination has ever seen.[19]

According to contemporaries, their work was marked by powerful results. This is attributed to the Moravians' understanding of the role of ongoing, faithful intercession, the "spirit of prayer" and the results these brought to the work of crosscultural ministry. Though many historians like to call William Carey the father of the modern mission movement, I believe the Moravians and Zinzendorf himself deserve this distinction, because they were sending laborers to difficult places fifty years before Carey went to India.

Just as we need to develop a Bible study plan, we need to plan for intercessory prayer. This includes setting aside a place for intercession in a location conducive to drawing near to the Lord—an inner chamber to meet with God. David Brainerd, message bearer to the American Indians in the 1700s, made the open woods his prayer chamber. He spent hours and entire days in the woods alone in deep burden and travail for the Indians. Hudson Taylor, the great message bearer to China in the 1800s, often made a riverboat his prayer chamber as he traveled from town to town. Praying Hyde (John Hyde) of India had a special room dedicated to daily communion with God.

My personal inner chamber is my home office in the early morning. Additionally, we have a Global Harvest Prayer Room in our SVM2 Equipping Center in Chiang Mai, which is dedicated to seeking God for global harvest. This room often becomes my inner chamber. There I draw near to God in worship and intercession for the nations.

Message bearers are meant to engage *diligently* in a faithful intercessory prayer life. The opposite of diligence is laziness. Laziness is a plague among believers that wars against our ability to develop disciplines related to the inner life. Diligence was important to Jesus, Paul and Peter, as all three emphasized its cultivation in every area of life. Diligence includes earnestness, zeal and carefulness (Hebrews 4:11; 2 Timothy 2:15). We take care to consistently prepare ourselves for effective intercessory prayer by deliberately working it into our schedules.

OUR RELATIONSHIP WITH GOD MATTERS

The prophet Amos declared, "Surely the Lord GOD does nothing, unless He reveals His secret to His servants the prophets" (Amos 3:7). As we have seen, God is passionate about relationship with his people. Human beings are created to enjoy intimate relationship with God. According to this verse, God will rarely act apart from revealing his plans to disciples who seek closeness with him. It is not pleasing to God if we spend some time in prayer and then go off and act as we choose. God is after disciples cultivating their obedience and character in secret as they grow in him. These are in the process of becoming effective intercessors.

The key prerequisite of effective intercession is intimate fellowship with Jesus. Apart from heart-level closeness, God does not reveal his secrets, which is the initial step of the prayer cycle in the first place. We do not serve a fatalistic God, distant and refusing to relate to us. God involves his people in the process of moving his plans and purposes toward their ultimate consummation. We engage in intercession based on what is revealed in his written Word and made known by the Spirit.

A biblical example of God revealing his purposes to those he is close to, provoking them to intercession, is Abraham's experience with the angels coming to destroy Sodom and Gomorrah. The Lord told Abraham what he intended to do to Sodom and Gomorrah based on their wickedness and his perfect justice. Because of Abraham's relationship with God and what God was preparing him to become, God told Abraham his plans.

Then the men rose from there and looked toward Sodom, and Abraham went with them to send them on the way. And the LORD said, "Shall I hide from Abraham what I am doing, since Abraham shall surely become a great and mighty nation, and all the nations of the earth shall be blessed in him? For I

> have known him, in order that he may command his children
> and his household after him, that they keep the way of the
> LORD, to do righteousness and justice, that the LORD may
> bring to Abraham what He has spoken to him." And the LORD
> said, "Because the outcry against Sodom and Gomorrah is
> great, and because their sin is very grave, I will go down now
> and see whether they have done altogether according to the
> outcry against it that has come to Me; and if not, I will know."
> (Genesis 18:16-21)

Abraham was moved to intercede for the righteous in Sodom and
Gomorrah, who would be wiped out with the wicked. God was
pleased with this response. Abraham began asking God to hold
back his just judgment if he could find fifty righteous people living
in the city. Abraham continued the intercession process until he
stopped at asking for God to stay judgment if he could find ten
righteous. God did not find even ten righteous people, because he
brought judgment on the city. Yet he did have the angels escort Lot
and his family out of the town—a result of Abraham's intercession.

Some struggle with the idea of God changing his mind. God is
omniscient, and his foreknowledge of every circumstance is complete. Would he decide to act and then change his mind from what
he, the sovereign God, planned to do? God's justice is required
unless there is repentance and a cleansing of sin by blood. The cities
of Sodom and Gomorrah deserved God's justice, as they consistently broke moral laws written into creation itself. Yet the tender
mercy in God's heart moved him to seek a way around this problem.
His purpose was mercy, and to withhold judgment, which is why
he provoked Abraham to intercede.

If God finds intercessors asking him to change his mind, he
sometimes does so, because he has set up his kingdom in partnership with his church. Apart from believers seeking God's face to

hold back judgment, a variety of judgments for sin and wickedness are inevitable.

Even if God finds intercessors, that's no guarantee he'll relent. God has built eternal laws into creation. Human sin brings God's judgment and death, while confession, repentance and restitution bring his mercy.[20] When wickedness is confessed, cleansed by the blood of Jesus and put away, God's judgment is held back. Apart from true repentance, judgment must come. God's justice isn't from a harsh desire to obliterate people, but according to laws of morality written into the fabric of the universe. Through perfect righteousness, God has provided a way of escape from such judgment through the shed blood of Jesus. But he will not force a person, family, ethnic group or nation to choose that way.

I'm not referring to God's end-time judgments, as those are set, but to specific, time-oriented judgments affecting individual people, groups, cities, nations and so on. God has ordained judgment to be withheld and mercy and grace extended through the intercession of his people in order to draw as many as possible to himself.

CONDITIONS OF INTERCESSORY PRAYER

What does intercession that releases Jesus' authority on earth look like? It has nothing to do with a person's personality, speaking skills or ability to project loudly in prayer meetings. Effective intercession has faith at its core. Trusting the unseen God is the cornerstone of a message bearer's life of faith. We deepen dependence on God in daily, practical situations. Nowhere is this more real than in our prayer lives. Intercessory prayer is holding fast to God, not letting go until he answers. Jacob wrestling with the angel in Genesis 32 is a wonderful picture of appropriate tenacity in intercession. We need to ask God to give a vision of the seriousness of intercession and what is at stake as we engage in it.

Effectiveness in intercessory prayer includes aligning with

certain conditions. Besides coming to God in the right spirit, attitude and motive, there are at least five additional conditions to see answers through intercession:[21]

1. Depending on the righteousness and work of Jesus as our only mediator before the Father and our only claim for blessing.

2. Turning from all known sin. The Lord will not hear the prayers of those consciously holding sin in their hearts.

3. Trusting in God's Word backed by his covenant with his people. Failure to believe God's ability to keep his promises is fatal to effective prayer.

4. Laying our own will aside and asking in line with his will—not seeking our own reputation, honor or riches through prayer.

5. Faithfully continuing in prayer by committing to wait on God and for God. We keep asking, seeking and knocking, without giving up.

WHAT DO WE PRAY?

In the Gospels, Jesus teaches his disciples *to* pray and *how* they should pray. Yet he seldom mentions *what* to pray. Generally, he leaves the *what* to our sense of need and the leading of the Spirit. But in the following verses Jesus directs our attention to a prayer focal point. Matthew wrote in his Gospel, "When [Jesus] saw the multitudes, He was moved with compassion for them, because they were weary and scattered, like sheep having no shepherd." Then Jesus said, "The harvest truly is plentiful, but the laborers are few. Therefore pray the Lord of the harvest to send out laborers into His harvest" (Matthew 9:37-38). After Jesus was moved with compassion for the multitudes, he directed his disciples to pray for effective laborers to be raised. He felt the pain of huge crowds in complete darkness with no one to speak truth to them. With a view of the abundant harvest to come and knowing the need for laborers to reap that harvest, we wholeheartedly seek him for the right kinds of laborers to be raised en masse.

This is a challenge to the modern church. It's generally uncommon to pray for laborers, because we don't feel the compassion or the burden Jesus feels for the lost around the world. Thousands of ethnic groups have little exposure to a powerful gospel witness and are ripe for spiritual harvest, but few disciples feel the pressing need to reap this harvest. We seldom feel the burden of the shepherdless millions wandering in darkness. Jesus, however, understood the nature of intercession and its importance in supplying necessary workers of high spiritual quality to serve the unreached and unengaged.

We need to stand in faith, asking the Lord, who rules the harvest, to send abundant, empowered laborers in answer to prayer. Through them, we ask the Lord to reap the countless fields ready for harvest. To engage in this sort of intense intercession, we need a growing empowerment of the Spirit.

Our staff in Chiang Mai spends an hour each morning in corporate prayer in our Global Harvest Prayer Room for a different country. We daily invite the Lord to show us what country he is leading us to pray for. Then we pray for spiritual awakening in that national church and growth among believers, that they would live with abandoned devotion to Jesus. Next, we pray for that national church to align with God's purpose in the Great Commission, becoming a strong sending body. Third, we pray for unreached and unengaged people groups within that nation to respond to the witness of Jesus. It's a powerful time of cooperating with what the Spirit is seeking to do in these nations.

In this practice, the most powerful tool in intercession is praying the Word of God. The Bible is the greatest prayer manual, yet most of us have not connected with it in that way. A Scripture relating to the subject of our prayers can preface almost every individual prayer. In this way, we can be assured we're praying according to the will of God, because we're praying the very Word of God. This practice ignites spiritual authority as we pray God's Word over believers, churches and the unreached.[22]

WHAT HAPPENS IN THE HEAVENS?

Jesus' words in Matthew 11:12 are key to understanding the power of effective intercessory prayer: "And from the days of John the Baptist until now the kingdom of heaven suffers violence, and the violent take it by force." The term *violence* in this context means "tearing." Jesus was saying that when John came onto the scene, something shifted in the heavenly realm, and a tearing took place. The shift was the transition from the previous age of the law and prophets to the current gospel age, as John faithfully preached a brand-new message: "The kingdom of God is at hand!"[23]

The doorway was opened for human beings to enter God's family through repentance and through trusting in Jesus' blood for salvation. Cultural and societal transformation in families, cities, ethnic groups and nations was now possible. The tearing unleashed spiritual power, which was manifested in Jesus and the disciples when they were sent out to preach, heal the sick and bring deliverance to those oppressed by the devil. Jesus taught that this age would be characterized by these kingdom manifestations.

At the end of Matthew 11:12, we receive an invitation to participate in the process by tearing the heavenly realm ourselves—not by physical force, but spiritually through intercessory prayer. The word *force* refers to spiritual seizing. This is done by cooperating with God in intercession and inviting his kingdom dynamics into others' circumstances. We engage with all our hearts (with zeal and fervency, not passivity), enabling spiritual power to be manifested among unreached ethnic groups for the glory of Jesus.

8

Cooperating with God's
Twofold Purpose

Spiritual Key # 7

The book of Jonah provides insight into the two highest priorities on the heart of God: (1) forming his people in the likeness of Jesus, and (2) restoring a broken and hurting world through his body. Cooperating in these two purposes is an essential spiritual key for thriving as God's message bearers, who often make mistakes in these areas.

The book of Jonah is important to the body of Christ. This little volume has the capacity to transform our lives in a multitude of areas. God is preparing his body to reap a massive global harvest of peoples from every tribe, tongue and nation under heaven. Preparation for this includes millions of disciples and thousands of churches and ministries cultivating these two highest priorities in our own lives. This is at the heart of the drama that unfolds in the book of Jonah.

The Father loves the Son. His greatest priority is conforming us into Jesus' likeness, so his ministry *to* a person is more important than his ministry *through* that person. In Jonah, God is as concerned with the change he wants to bring in Jonah as the change he desires in Nineveh. In his dealings with Jonah, God prepares Jonah's life for his purposes just as he prepares us. We often misunderstand or resist a process God uses to develop us (as Jonah did), simply because we aren't aware of his strategies.

While living in Istanbul, Kelly and I went through a painful season lasting about a year. It seemed disappointments and setbacks in our international work were constant. Our staff was struggling, and external crises were rampant. As we prayed for understanding, the Lord began teaching us his processes for maturing us. First, we recognized we were at war with a real enemy. In this war, we needed to be watchful and vigilant, operating in Jesus' delegated authority.

Second, he revealed that true ministry includes setbacks and disappointments. During this season, I read an article by a respected author and ministry leader in which he noted that he could not remember a day in the life of his ministry of more than thirty years that didn't include difficulties. Knowing that difficulties are normal in ministry and not something we alone were facing enabled us to stand in faith instead of succumb to discouragement. The Spirit built dependence on Jesus, conforming us to his likeness. Our dependence was not on us, a certain work or a particular ministry, but him alone.

Third, we came to understand that setbacks and disappointments, when reflected on and understood, can be a training tool in God's hand. Through them, he can lay deeper foundations and rootedness in him. Our goal tends to be production while God's goal is to conform us to Jesus' likeness. But often God has to tear down ideas of ministry success to build what he intends. In Kelly's and my season of difficulty, God showed us that he loves the journey and uses difficulties, and our responses to them, to develop holiness in us. Our job is to choose to walk in faithfulness and obedience.

GROWING IN HOLINESS

It's easy to forget that God is shaping his children in the likeness of Christ, known in theological terms as sanctification or holiness. As we cooperate with God's intent of making us holy, he reverses the effects of the fall in every believer's life.[1] As disciples, holiness is meant to be our identity as a spotless bride. This is God's intent for his body and promise to his Son.

It's a contradiction for a disciple to tolerate continual impurity. God has put it into every believer to be holy, but this doesn't happen without a battle. Soon after being born again, we become conscious of the real battle within—the clash between our flesh and the Spirit of God. Each seeks the upper hand. And the flesh frequently wins. Learning the ways of God in overcoming our sinful natures is essential. Many hear of victory over sin through Jesus' blood and understand it doctrinally, but they have never experienced it, so they doubt such victory is possible.

In Romans 7–8, Paul recounted his own struggles with this. In chapter 7, he wrote of his anguish and failure, while chapter 8 revealed the Holy Spirit providing victory through Jesus' blood. Paul had tried to overcome sin through his own effort. He recognized the fruitlessness of this endeavor and saw the Spirit's ability to deliver him from sin when he yielded. This is God's prescribed method for walking in victory over the sinful nature.

Living in victory includes internalizing two sides of Jesus' work: we're "in Christ," and Christ is "in us." The nature of Christianity motivates believers to receive from God. Our inheritance isn't in what we do for God but in what he has made available by historical fact. Ephesians 3:6 tells us we're heirs with Christ, partakers of the promise. Through trusting Jesus' work on the cross and by his resurrection, we enter into that inheritance with him.

First, we have been placed "in Christ." Believers have a new status before God based solely on the work of Christ on our behalf. When we receive Jesus' work through his death and resurrection, our status before God changes from an enemy to being accepted, forgiven and beloved. This status, neither earned nor attained, makes us recipients of all Jesus endured. We are now "in him." We have died with him and been raised to life in him. Resurrection "in Christ" means that when God looks at us, he doesn't see our stains and failures, but the eternal blood of Jesus.

Second, Christ "in us" gives us power to live worthy of him, bent on his purposes. Christ in us gives us his power. Jesus' sacrifice on the cross satisfied God's justice. Jesus now has deposited this same dynamic life in us. Efforts to be holy come up short every time, but his life in us enables us to enjoy victory over sin. We activate victory by receiving the shedding of his blood in our circumstances as an always available gift. This isn't mere doctrine; it's meant to be daily walked out. It is the ongoing good news of the gospel for every disciple.

THE PROCESS OF PRUNING

The battle between flesh and Spirit is pronounced as we serve as God's message bearers. In crosscultural situations, our inner desires are more apparent. If we're prone to anger, people of differing values, habits and activities incite more anger in us. If lust is a problem, the stresses of another environment heighten our battle. If self-centeredness is an issue, the challenges of another culture will inevitably accentuate our overinflated ego.

To help develop us in holiness, God prunes us. Jesus teaches, "Every branch in Me that does not bear fruit He takes away; and every branch that bears fruit He prunes, that it may bear more fruit" (John 15:2). God's pruning can be equated with testing. As we bear fruit he prunes (tests), and responding positively to his tests produces more fruit in us.

Pruning (or testing) is painful. When a branch is pruned, it's cut. Thankfully, it is cutting to produce greater inward and outward spiritual expansion in the future. As Kelly and I reflected on our painful season in Istanbul, we began to see the pruning hand of our loving

Father. He was testing us, cutting us back, to bring more fruitfulness later. He did this out of love for us, to develop holiness in us.

Many aren't aware that the pruning is from God. This was initially true for Kelly and me. We had been taught about pruning but had not made the truths our own. We sometimes confused God's pruning with an attack of the evil one. The enemy tempts us, but God never tempts us, though he will test us in many areas. The tests aren't primarily for him; he knows us inside and out. They reveal areas *to us* in which we need to grow.

We find two biblical responses to God's tests: positive and negative. A test emerges based on a person's character. If someone fails to perceive the incident as being from God or deliberately goes against inner convictions, God restricts her inner growth and brings the same test around later. With a positive response, the person recognizes the incident as from God and chooses to stand on her inner convictions. God blesses the positive response by bringing spiritual expansion within and without the person's life.

GOD'S TESTING

Every biblical character underwent God's testing. Not one was immune. David had a great purpose in God, and the Lord took him through painful seasons to reveal his pride to prepare him to be the king God wanted. Paul was tested throughout his ministry by a thorn in his flesh. God pruned him, resulting in the advance of the gospel among the Gentiles. Testing is always meant to mature and expand a person spiritually.

God does the same with us. The Bible says that our hearts are deceptively wicked. What we want in life and ministry rarely produces deeper holiness. It generally hurts us. But allowing God to have his way produces a heart after him—even when it involves pain. Left to ourselves, we tend to harm ourselves in untold ways. In contrast, submitting to God's ways produces a rich result over time, leading us in challenging ways to conform us to the likeness of Jesus.

As already mentioned, in my early years in ministry, the Lord gave substantial divine guidance concerning my calling and ministry mandate. In my spiritual immaturity, I thought these things would immediately materialize as I set my hand to them. Instead, God used his guidance to test my heart. Would I trust him to bring his plans to pass in me and through me in his timing? Over the past fifteen years, I've periodically wondered if I discerned God's guidance correctly. In those moments of doubt, the Lord's response has often been to lead me to Psalm 105:19: "Until the time that his word came to pass, the word of the LORD tested him." This is a reference to Joseph's God-given dreams and his twenty-two years waiting for them to be fulfilled. God had shown him what he intended to bring to pass, and Joseph needed to trust God's wisdom in preparing him to live under the weight of those purposes. It's the same for us as we live according to the leading of the Lord, being prepared for the fulfillment of his promises.

Have you considered King Saul's role as David's training tool? What if Saul had not rejected David and sought to kill him? Would David have developed the same inner strength? Would David have learned to wait on God? Would he have had an unshakable confidence in God? God will always allow a Saul, as a tool of testing, when he is training a David. This is often the case with younger leaders. God puts them under an authority that appears to them to be hindering their development in ministry. Instead, the authority is being used to test them and develop holiness as they respond correctly. Will they submit to God's will or manipulate the situation for their own gain? This was David's temptation throughout Saul's reign.

AREAS GOD TESTS

Throughout life and ministry, God brings several forms of testing in the following areas. It helps us to be aware of them so we can respond to them positively instead of resisting.

- Obedience to God, his written Word and the leading of the Spirit
- Hearing his voice, through both the Bible and his Spirit
- Faithfulness with ministry tasks
- Receiving guidance
- Honoring spiritual authority
- Use of words
- Use of time, money, energies and relationships
- What we look at, listen to and give attention to
- Attitudes toward material possessions
- Each of the nine fruits of the Spirit

Are we looking for affirmation from others or from the Father? People-pleasing is a common area of bondage message bearers fall into. We subtly seek honor and favor from people instead of from God. John 5:44 sheds important light on this issue: "How can you believe, who receive honor from one another, and do not seek the honor that comes from the only God." Jesus connects our proneness to look to others for honor with unbelief. People-pleasing dulls our spiritual capacities, specifically our trust in and dependence on God, as we look to others for approval. Conversely, receiving affirmation from God cultivates stronger trust. Do we look for honor from those we see or from the unseen God?[2]

Human beings are easily affected by what others say. God is watching to see if we're more concerned with our reputation than with obeying him. A foundation for cultivating spiritual authority is overcoming concern for reputation in obedience to God. Kelly and I are both graduates of Fuller Seminary in Pasadena. In response to the Lord's leading in our lives, we began to raise financial support for serving the nations. One of our well-meaning relatives remarked, "You two are well educated and could get wonderful jobs here in America, but instead you're going around asking for money." It hurt to be misunderstood and wrongly characterized, yet that gave us an opportunity to choose obedience over reputation.

PRODUCING PATIENCE

The hardest tests seem to be related to developing patience. In the Bible, patience is often connected with living in the fullness of God. James wrote, "But let patience have its perfect work, that you may be perfect and complete, lacking nothing" (James 1:4).

Paul prayed for the Colossian believers, asking God to spiritually strengthen them to "walk worthy of the Lord, fully pleasing Him, being fruitful in every good work and increasing in the knowledge of God; strengthened with all might, according to His glorious power, for all patience and longsuffering with joy" (Colossians 1:10-11). These five traits Paul prayed are wonderful in and of themselves, and it's good to consider how to grow in each of these areas. However, notice that they serve to prepare believers to be "patient and longsuffering with joy."

Patience is more than just having a good attitude as we wait in traffic. It's actively waiting for the promises of God to come to pass. The psalms regularly mention the discipline of waiting on God. This includes holding fast to what he has promised in his Word and by his Spirit. It might involve a spouse, a ministry, a financial issue, an ethnic group or healing of an illness. Does unbelief and doubt start to creep in? Do we actively wait a while and then quit when nothing happens? This reveals a lack of patience. God develops patience to make us like Jesus; he roots out the hurry within. We live with urgency for the kingdom, and that draws us to ask God about each step, to seek to hear from him about each undertaking. This requires increasing patience, which we grow in as it's imparted by the Spirit.

THE GOSPEL OF THE KINGDOM

God's second-highest priority, revealed vividly in the book of Jonah, is his passion for drawing millions into relationship with Christ. God's heart burned with love for the Ninevites as those who "did not know their right hand from their left." We seek to fulfill God's desire by ordering our lives around his purpose of providing a powerful, culturally relevant witness of the gospel of the kingdom among every ethnic group. Cooperating with this calling is a response of fervent love for Jesus.

We're familiar with Jesus' words in Matthew 24:14: "And this gospel of the kingdom will be preached in all the world as a witness to all the nations [ethnic groups], and then the end will come." What exactly is the "gospel of the kingdom"? Is it the same as the gospel of eternal salvation, or is it more multifaceted? Many have reduced the gospel to the message of salvation being spread to every ethnic group so that Jesus returns. But Jesus is referring to much more. The message of eternal salvation is the gospel's bedrock, yet the gospel is not limited to that.

The core of the Christian message is the presence and power of the kingdom of God at work among us.[3] To put it another way, it's the presence of the government of God experienced on earth in its fullness. Jesus taught the kingdom of God more than any other subject in the Gospels, and there is much more to it than meets the eye. The kingdom of God is both a present hidden reality (in this age) and a coming hope (in the age to come). This biblical hope isn't merely focused on individual salvation—salvation from the guilt and eternal penalty of sin. It's the corporate salvation of the people of God living on the earth and their deliverance from all evil—spiritual, social, political and physical.[4]

God's kingly vision is to rule with justice and authority over individual lives, families, local cities, ethnic groups, geopolitical entities and the whole earth. This will literally happen and be ushered in through the second coming of Christ. To communicate the gospel of the kingdom is primarily to teach God's rightful leadership over all created order. The gospel of the kingdom focuses on Jesus' loving commitment to restore broken fellowship with God the king among all human beings as they confess sin, believe in his Son and do the will of the Father. It refers to the potential of all society being transformed as people corporately submit to the leadership, values and principles of the king. So, as message bearers who apply Jesus' teachings of the kingdom by teaching all ethnic groups, we affect our surroundings significantly.

THE KINGDOM'S PROGRESSION

God's purpose in creation was to fill the earth with people who would have unhindered fellowship with him. His desire for intimate relationship was his primary motivation. This would take place as his heavenly kingdom became manifest on earth. And this is what Adam and Eve were brought into. The garden of Eden was the perfect manifestation of the kingdom of God in operation on the earth. It was God's intent for his people for all time.

Yet there was another kingdom seeking to establish its reign: the kingdom of Satan. Satan influenced Adam and Eve to choose sin rather than obey God.[5] God set up his kingdom with free will, so every human being could freely choose whom to follow. Throughout the Old Testament, the prophets understood the kingdom on earth as a reality not readily seen in the present. The prophets looked to a future hope partially manifested through Jesus' first coming, continuing throughout the present age and being fully established at his second coming and on into the age to come.

Jesus came onto the scene declaring, "The kingdom of heaven is at hand." He exemplified the bent of children of the kingdom: committed obedience to the king and a desire above all else to do his will. Through his sacrificial death, Jesus broke the power of Satan, sin and death, was resurrected, and ascended to sit on his throne as king at the right hand of God. The way was opened for the beginning of the transformation of creation as believers willingly chose to put their lives under his governmental leadership.

Through the outpouring of the Spirit at Pentecost, the dynamic influence was provided for the kingdom of God to once again be realized through born-again believers. Yet we don't often see the transformative power of the kingdom in effect as God intended. A partial reason is that we limit the effects of the kingdom to eternal salvation instead of including God's plan of delivering society from evil as the body of Christ yields to his governmental leadership. We want to see this in an increasing measure in the present age while recognizing that the fullness takes place in the age to come.

At Jesus' second coming, the full weight of the kingdom of God will be brought to bear on the earth. Jesus will literally set up his kingly reign, and all will be subject to him. He will overhaul the infrastructures of the world along the lines of his kingdom intention. The earth will be fully restored to its original intention, similar to what Adam and Eve experienced with God in the garden.

We long for the functioning of the kingdom as intended in the heart of God. When message bearers proclaim "the gospel of the kingdom," we raise the vision of Jesus as king and rightful leader over all creation. And people turn from an old life of waywardness (sin) and follow Jesus in new life.

SUFFERING AS A MEANS OF SPREADING THE GOSPEL

The New Testament teaches suffering itself as a means for producing fruit among unreached ethnic groups, cities and nations. Much emphasis has been placed on suffering as a result of communicating the gospel, yet it's much more than that. Jesus understood that the kingdom of God is actualized as weak people embrace a lifestyle of suffering. His entire life and ministry embraced this truth, and he modeled it while teaching, "Unless a grain of wheat falls into the ground and dies, it remains alone; but if it dies, it produces much grain" (John 12:24).

Jesus was sent to suffer and die voluntarily to redeem (purchase) an innumerable number from all ethnic groups globally throughout history, while releasing power to transform society through his kingdom authority. Christ's victory was accomplished through suffering and death. Voluntary willingness to suffer is the *message* of the gospel, yet also our *method* in reaching people with Christ. We *receive his love* through his sufferings on the cross on our behalf. We then *embrace his sufferings* as a means of producing a harvest among unreached ethnic groups.[6]

It's common among believers to think that, since Jesus shed his blood and died for us, we have been spared from suffering. It's true that Jesus' sacrifice in our place enables restored fellowship with the Father while cleansing and sanctifying us. Yet Jesus did not offer his life and shed his blood to protect us from sacrifice but to make the sacrifice of our own lives possible and even desirable. Another way to put it is that Jesus died not to free us *from* suffering but to free us *for* suffering. Many Scriptures throughout the Bible encapsulate this core concept of true Christianity. We walk out this truth by daily prioritizing the eternal over the temporal.

Multitudes of opportunities come our way to suffer for the kingdom. In late 2007, the Lord gave me a small taste of what many go through regularly in serving God. Thirteen message bearers and I were meeting in a hotel in a western city in Turkey known for its nationalism and dislike of people in our line of work. There is a law in Turkey that foreigners checking into hotels must present a passport. Not thinking, I had left my passport at home in Istanbul. On arrival to the hotel, I apologized to the receptionist for forgetting my passport. She responded graciously, saying, "No problem." Our group went on with our meetings, thinking nothing of it.

Later that evening, a knock came to our conference room door, and the Jandarma (local police) demanded I accompany them to police headquarters, a thirty-minute drive away. We asked what the problem was. They informed us, "This man doesn't have his passport." The officer knew it sounded ridiculous as the words tumbled from his mouth. Something else was going on. Two from our group joined me, and we were escorted to waiting police cars. In the car, the highest-ranking officer started questioning me about why I was in the country, what my work was, where I got money and so on—common questions message bearers in countries like Turkey learn to have ready answers for. I gave my "story" without flinching, answering only what was asked and nothing more.

The officer became visibly agitated and flustered. In rage, he fumed, "I think your entire group is here to teach your religion, and we don't want you here." We immediately grasped what was going on. Since Turkey officially has "freedom of religion," the authorities could not legally hold me. However, they could hold me for failing to show my passport at check-in. This was an excuse to make life difficult for people like us. I was held at the police headquarters for more than twelve hours until my passport was hand-delivered from Istanbul.

God uses seeds of suffering to bring an eventual harvest for his kingdom. In every circumstance, we respond by "dying" and letting go or by holding on and potentially hindering future fruit. A harvest comes where seeds fall to the ground and die. All believers are called to tread this path, and those serving as message bearers among the unreached have many opportunities to do so.

In April 2007, about a month after my family first arrived in Turkey, three message bearers (two from a Turkish background and one German) were brutally murdered for their faith in the south-central city of Malatya. Five nineteen-year-olds had been hired to kill these "infidels." It came out later through the trial that governmental authorities fairly high up the chain of command had given the green light for the killings. The number of Turkish evangelical believers is quite small (about four thousand), and every believer was personally affected by the tragedy. Most knew at least one of the three quite well.

About a week prior to the killings, I had met with a Turkish lay leader in one of the churches in Istanbul. I asked what she thought it would take to see spiritual breakthrough in her country. She responded, "Many of us being imprisoned and even dying for our faith." Obviously, she had no idea what was about to take place, but she knew the principle Jesus was getting at when he spoke of the grain of wheat falling to the ground and dying. The murders provided a powerful testimony of forgiveness, as the Turkish media carried the story of the responses of the wives and a fiancée of the three. As they chose love over hatred, forgiveness over bitterness, the essence of the gospel was publicly declared firsthand. Incidentally, these were the first Christian martyrs in the Turkish body of believers.

Progressing in this understanding requires a new paradigm, a new perspective on suffering and martyrdom. Gaining God's viewpoint on this precious grace enables us to no longer see suffering as mere drudgery. Instead, we find opportunity to grow in Christlikeness, producing fruit among the unreached.

Martyrdom is increasing as we move closer to the second coming of Christ. God is using increased suffering among believers as part of his strategy for producing the greatest harvest ever seen among the unreached. Loyalty and allegiance to Christ are necessary and in some cases mean loss of life. The world sees death as the end and the greatest enemy. In biblical theology, physical death is never the end or the enemy as we embrace an eternal perspective. As disciples, we internalize Jesus' perspective on death, not a worldly one.

The first-century church progressed among hostile ethnic groups by publicly communicating the message, denouncing false gods, calling people to the true God, painting a picture of the kingdom of God and boldly explaining the way of salvation. Persecution came not because they were unwise in their gospel expressions but because the nature of the message stood in direct conflict with their communities. Acts of bold proclamation drew multitudes to Christ as hearers marveled at the disciples' willingness to risk all for the sake of the message shared. Multitudes determined the message bearers' words to be true because of this. The coming of the Holy Spirit at Pentecost (Acts 2) produced bold witnesses. We must pray for a fresh infusion of this anointed characteristic across the global mission movement.

I was a speaker at a large student mission conference sponsored by Nigeria Fellowship of Evangelical Students (NIFES), the Nigerian national movement of the International Fellowship of Evangelical Students (IFES). The organizers had planned a challenge portion for the last evening. Mike Adegbile, then national director of NIFES, asked me to give the challenge. He encouraged me to make it quite difficult, saying, "Nigerians are emotional and will respond to most challenges. You must set it apart to get a real response."

I told the conference participants, "God is calling Nigerians to take the gospel to all West and North Africa. This will mean engaging Muslim-dominated lands, where it's illegal to become a Christian. It will mean engaging Arab Africans, who generally despise black Africans. It will mean a percentage of you losing your lives as martyrs for God's kingdom. Who will respond to the beckoning of the Spirit to be Jesus' hands and feet? Who will come to the altar?"

My eyes were closed, not because I was praying, but because I didn't want to see no one coming forward and the altar area empty. I thought, *Has Mike set me up to fail?* After several moments of waiting on the Lord, I slowly glanced at the altar area to see hundreds of young people slowly streaming forward with tears rolling down their cheeks. By the end, more than four hundred students of the roughly seven thousand at the conference had committed themselves as message bearers after counting the cost.

THE APOSTOLIC MESSAGE

There is a call rising for apostolic message bearers to reclaim the mantle of spiritual authority. What does this mean? A return to New Testament focal points as to what the gospel is and how that message is integrated into the lives of new disciples. Often our message has appeared to be watered down; it's sometimes unclear what the biblical essence of the gospel is when listening to those speaking on its behalf. I've been in meetings where leaders discuss why the early church saw much fruitfulness and why we lack it. Could it be we have gotten away from the core message preached in the New Testament in favor of an "easier" or "more tolerable" message?

Through a study of the book of Acts, and more specifically several of Paul's letters to churches, we find core elements of the message the early church preached. God is the same yesterday, today and forever. His Word never changes and is always the source of truth, revealing the power, love and authority of the eternal and preexistent God incarnated among humanity. The message communicated should be the same as in Paul's day, with the addition not of content but of culturally relevant communication tools.

What makes a witness "apostolic"? It isn't a style of communication or personality type. These do not matter. An apostolic witness emphasizes the rule of God over all created order and the sending of his Son as a man. Only in sending the uncreated and eternal Christ as a man could God remove the sin of rebellious humanity through his sacrificial death, satisfying the debt of guilt before his throne and restoring the lost privileges of living in vital relationship with the Father. The apostolic message is Jesus crucified and resurrected, and a person believing with his heart, confessing with his mouth and turning from all known sin as the doorway to relationship with a holy God.

CORE ELEMENTS

We find one of the clearest summaries of the apostolic message in Paul's first letter to the Thessalonians. The message contains the following critical elements:

- There is one true and living God who rules over all. Idolatry is sinful and must be forsaken.

- The wrath of God is revealed against the wicked for their impurity.

- The judgment will come suddenly and unexpectedly.

- Jesus, the Son of God, given over to death and raised from the dead, is the only savior from the wrath of God.

- The kingdom of Jesus is now available, and all are invited to enter and influence society according to kingdom standards.

- Those who believe and turn to God expect the coming of the Savior, who will return from heaven to receive them.

- Meanwhile their life must be pure, useful and watchful. To that end, God has given them the Holy Spirit.[7]

Often our message doesn't reflect these foundational elements. Some are regularly spoken of as "the gospel," yet too many are strangely absent. Could we be seeing weaker disciples because of our failure to communicate the full gospel in the manner shown to us by Paul? The apostolic message is God acting in love, providing an escape from the inheritance of sin. It speaks directly and personally to every individual, family and ethnic group that they have rejected God by not believing he sent Jesus to rescue them from sinful depravity. The full gospel calls people to flee the wrath coming upon those apart from

Christ. This fleeing is done by "hiding" in the shelter of Jesus' blood.

This kind of proclamation is marked by boldness. Being bold doesn't mean speaking loudly and being dramatic—or speaking softly and being subtle; it's the Spirit through us doing the work. Boldness is a reflection of the inner confidence God has given to those sent to sow his kingdom; it's an expectation that results will follow. Boldness is often subtly understood as being harsh or rough, but true boldness speaks truth with tenderness and love. God has initiated the process, wanting to reach people through a message of transformation for all. We follow him to the ends of the earth with inner boldness ablaze in our hearts.

TOUGH LOVE

Paul's posture with the Gentiles was always sympathy and love. Yet he would never be misunderstood as condoning idolatry, suggesting all ways lead to God or tolerating wicked practices. Paul made clear what was required of hearers. He motivated them to turn from wrongdoing, repent to God and believe in Jesus as the only sacrifice restoring what they were created for. Paul took an uncompromising stand against sin and its deadly effects. The apostolic message is the power of sin to kill the spirit, heart and soul, separating us from God. Conversely, the powerful blood of Christ removes that sin.

A message bearer in Turkey was discipling a new Turkish believer. The convert seemed genuine in his desire to follow Christ. After some months, it became known he was continuing to live with his girlfriend. The message bearer lovingly confronted the man, asking if he knew Jesus' teaching to abstain from sexual activity outside of marriage. The man confided he had no idea. The message bearer opened the Bible and showed him God's thoughts on the subject. The new believer willingly asked the girlfriend to move out and stopped having sexual activity with her. The message bearer was loving but firm in teaching the new believer. Surprisingly, many message bearers don't confront, in favor of helping establish a new believer first.

A MISAPPLIED DOCTRINE

Scripture warns that the number of teachers and preachers who are "false" will increase. They teach what people want to hear and stray from God's truth (2 Timothy 4:3). We see this escalating in many circles of the body of Christ, even among message bearers. "False teachers" aren't evil-looking people with horns blaspheming Jesus as Lord; we need to get out of the mind-set that false teachers are apparent because they blatantly teach falsehoods. They generally speak orthodox Christian doctrine but with a spin.

The scriptural issue false teachers in the New Testament were generally guilty of was antinomianism. They minimized grace by saying people could obtain forgiveness from God apart from repenting and putting the sin away. This falsehood was all over the ancient world and is equally prevalent today. It's the preaching of Christian liberty with a wrong application, giving believers and unbelievers alike the impression that Jesus forgives while we continue in willful sin. It's an affront to the justice of God and the cross of Christ. It also encourages mistaken security before God as people continue in sin deliberately and feel comfortable doing so, believing God is okay with it.

God does forgive each time we sincerely confess, as his mercy and grace are never exhausted. Yet the apostle John affirms that continuing in sin apart from gaining a measure of victory reveals a problem in a person's life in Christ. John doesn't mince words; he says this person is not a believer (1 John 3:4-9). This has nothing to do with perfection but with a heart response of sincerely wanting to obey God. On the one side is a believer with a heart for God who periodically falls into a sin. She genuinely hates her sin and cries out to God in repentance. She fights against it each time, not content to resign herself to defeat. She recognizes sin's corroding effects, sees its grip on her life and chooses to flee from it by crying out to God in heartfelt confession. To her, God will give victory in time.

On the other side is a believer who has tried fighting against a specific area of sin but it continues to dominate him. He is emotionally and spiritually tired and buys into the idea that living in victory is impossible, so he stops trying. Giving up on God's vision of holiness, he favors what he considers a more realistic Christian existence. He says he loves Jesus and that God forgives him, understanding the situation. His belief is reinforced by the common message that God forgives, while the requirement of repentance and putting away sin is minimized.

Message bearers do not have the right to offer forgiveness apart from true repentance. We bring people to God on his terms of salvation, through the shed blood of the Son of God. We cooperate with God's standards, calling people to rise to them. The apostolic message is that Jesus forgives sin as we repent and turn from that sin, and he empowers us to put it away by the power of his blood.

A way of overcoming this falsehood is a recommitment on the part of message bearers to study, understand and emphasize the power of the blood of Christ. There are so many layers of truth wrapped up in the blood. It's the centerpiece of reconciliation with God, as it overcomes the awful effects sin has wrought since the fall. We often rightly emphasize the effects of sin on us, forgetting its more substantial role on God. The love of God for humanity has never changed, but sin made it impossible for God to allow human beings to have fellowship with him.

It's an unalterable law that sin must bring forth sorrow and death. Sin is contempt of the authority of God. It's determined opposition to a holy God, and as a result, according to the laws of the universe, it awakens the wrath of God. But the blood of Jesus has been shed. For those receiving it, sin has been brought to nothing. The holiness of God no longer terrifies us. God is pleased and filled with exuberant love as he looks on those who accept his sacrifice of blood.

The Moravians (discussed in chapter 7) put substantial emphasis on the power of the blood. Zinzendorf became a student of the blood and derived extensive insight that stimulated the entire Moravian community in a significant way. We tend to understand the elementary benefits of the blood as the centerpiece of God's redemption, yet there is much more the Lord will teach about the power of Christ's blood to those who seek it.

THE WHOLE SPECTRUM OF JESUS

When someone tells me, "I believe in God!" I'm tempted to ask, "What God do you believe in?" Is he the true God of the Bible or a creation of our imaginations? We human beings live a large portion of our lives in our minds, which produce millions of images during both our waking and sleeping hours. We visualize what we anticipate and remember what has happened. Combined experiences and input from when we were children contribute to images and visualizations related to myriads of issues in our lives today.

Message bearers' concepts of God aren't immune to these images. We conjure up ideas based on our experiences, culture and environments. It's most comfortable to focus on particular attributes of God at the expense of others, thus creating gods of our own imaginations. Unless we replace these faulty concepts with applied truth, we have skewed images of God. More than ever, message bearers need to teach the whole counsel of God out of the reservoir of their own application.

Consider the two sides of Jesus' temperament. He is full of love, mercy, forgiveness and grace and equally absolutely holy. Many message bearers have a hard time communicating the two sides as both equally God. We naturally focus on one to the neglect of the other. Jesus' justice, wrath and judgment are to be understood and revered as much as his love, forgiveness and grace; his love and mercy motivate his justice. Teaching God's mercy alone implies that sin and holiness are secondary in the life of a disciple, while concentrating primarily on his judgment overlooks Jesus' eternal kindness to the repentant sinner. Message bearers must faithfully communicate the full spectrum of God found in Christ. Failure to do so produces disciples deficient in faith.

9

Understanding the Times
and Seasons of God

Spiritual Key # 8

My family and I arrived in Istanbul in March 2007. We had relocated from a Western city (London, Ontario) to Istanbul, a thriving international city of eighteen million people that literally bridges Europe and Asia and has Islamic roots and secular values. It was to be a central location for seeing national SVM2 alliances developed globally. The Lord had given us criteria for a base location, and Istanbul fit the bill: a global airport, a free democracy and predominantly Muslim. Living in such a location enabled us to be an example as we mobilized the body of Christ in different nations to serve the unreached and unengaged.

We got busy with the work of developing national SVM2 alliances through international networking and serving emerging mission movements. Over the first year, it became clear that developing the training center idea the Lord had spoken to us about (see chapter 6) was going to be more difficult than we'd expected, and we discerned it was not yet the season for it. God had a much different purpose for our four years in Turkey. If we hadn't discerned this early on, we might have caused much trouble for ourselves.

A spiritual key for thriving as God's message bearers is continuing to learn throughout life.[1] We embrace and partner with God in each season he brings, seeking to learn all we can. God leads us through seasons with specific purposes attached to them. Maintaining a learning posture is a primary way to steer clear of the natural tendency to plateau in our love for Jesus and his work.

The term "lifelong learning" doesn't merely refer to academic study, though there may be an important place for it. We learn from books, mentoring relationships (upward, downward and peer), the Bible, nature, movies, current events, news and much more. An essential question to ask in all of life is, "What is God trying to teach me through this?" Additionally, church and mission history teach principles we're wise to integrate into our ministry. It's true that if we do not consider history, we're doomed to repeat it. More than this, we're inspired as we consider those who went before us in faith. We learn vicariously through others' lives and experiences with God.

An important way we learn is through understanding God's use of various times and seasons. Several years ago, while studying the book of 1 Chronicles, I ran across a popular verse in chapter 12: "The sons of Issachar . . . had understanding of the times, to know what Israel ought to do" (v. 32). I was seeking God for clarity concerning what he was doing in the world. Though I knew generally what he was doing—tirelessly wooing and drawing people to himself—I wanted specifics. And he highlighted this Scripture to me. Here were the twelve tribes of Israel during the beginning of the reign of King David. God had given each tribe various strengths. The tribe of Issachar excelled in understanding the spiritual implications of the events taking place during the time they lived in and were able to instruct Israel in what to do. Our times require spiritual leaders to arise in droves with this same spirit of understanding.

Many message bearers do not feel we're living with spiritual understanding related to the events of the day and in our personal lives. As a result, we don't feel confident in instructing others on what should be done spiritually. The good news is that we can understand and that God wants us to seek wisdom. He doesn't hide understanding from us; instead, too few are wholeheartedly seeking it. God gives clarity and understanding to all who ask (and keep on asking), propelling us toward the fulfillment of the Great Commission.

UNDERSTANDING THE TIMES

The sons of Issachar understood the times because they knew the God in control of those times. They discerned his heart intent in the context of the bigger picture. This took time, effort and spiritual work on their part. Their discernment was the result of their hard work over many years of going deep with God, watching, listening and obeying his Word.

Within the space of twelve months in 2011, I found myself in two locations where some of the most large-scale human rights abuses of the past three hundred years took place. On the coast of Ghana, a few hours west of the capital, Accra, are huge slave fortresses, which were used in the slave trade from West Africa. Touring the inner halls and holding cells, and walking through the "point of no return"—a large doorway where slaves by the hundreds of thousands were marched to awaiting ships—moved me to tears. Though I personally was not involved in such activity, my American forefathers were.

As I walked the compound, I vicariously repented on behalf of those involved in the atrocities that destroyed centuries of generations, ripping families apart. A Ghanaian friend told me many Africans and African Americans return to the fortresses annually. It's there the family tree goes blank. They can often trace their family line as far back as the slave trade but no further, because records of who slaves were or where they came from were deliberately not kept. A sense of rootlessness set in and remains.

Near Krakow, Poland, is the notorious Auschwitz death camp,

where the Nazis systematically exterminated thousands of Poles, Russians and Jews in the early 1940s. Seeing firsthand the brutality of a people who subjugated another was overwhelming. I walked in the gas chambers where millions were told they were to receive showers, only to be systematically gassed. Viewing the barracks where many were tortured, starved and treated inhumanely so recently by a "civilized" country was shocking. The visit was deeply personal, as my maternal grandmother was Jewish. Her family had emigrated to the United States years before. I asked the tour guide if I, with a quarter Jewish blood, would have been rounded up had I lived during the early 1940s in Europe. She replied, "If the Nazis discovered your lineage, yes."

As I sought to understand why God had taken me to those two locations, he revealed more of his outlook on injustice. As I gained insight into God's character, I began to grasp the crucial role of the body of Christ in fighting global injustices. Generally, the church of the day in both these locations was silent. There were obvious exceptions in both William Wilberforce (fighting the slave trade)[2] and Dietrich Bonhoeffer (standing defiantly against Nazism).[3] Most, however, went with the flow of society, forgetting the body of Christ's calling as a countercultural movement.

We don't want the same guilt in our day. Declaring the gospel of the kingdom means bringing the values and leadership of Christ over all created order to bear against injustices. Today, message bearers work to overcome modern-day slavery, teach the values of the kingdom, speak out against corrupt practices that enslave people in poverty, take a stand when those who have no voice are trampled on, and speak into a culture when its traditions and practices subjugate others in the name of "this is our way."

Message bearers' spiritual perspective is broadened as they see global and local events in the context of God's purposes and desires. This gets us out of a fishbowl mentality. We see the fingerprints of

God as he steadily moves redemptive history in a specific direction. This is a primary difference between disciples partnering with God in the big picture and those who do not.

STUDYING THE END TIMES

Becoming people who understand our times means growing in what the Bible says about the end times.[4] This involves not mere academic study but a prayerful search of the Scriptures while allowing God to illuminate truth regarding what is to come. Scripture seems to indicate that the body of Christ's role in the Great Commission is inextricably connected to what happens near the end. Every previous generation (including the first-century church) looked forward to the events of the end as motivation for what they engaged in during their own day.

Many believers appear to be afraid to study prayerfully what the Bible has to say about the end times. This seems to be rooted in a mistaken fear that the end times are too confusing to understand. The argument goes that with so many conflicting interpretations, we can't really know how to correctly interpret these descriptions of events. In my experience, this fear is unfounded. The Holy Spirit would not put such an important book as Revelation in the Bible if it were impossible to understand. The Bible is full of end-time prophecy both in the Old and New Testaments. We're meant to grasp the plan for our partnering with God in seeing these things actualized. Studying the end times isn't as confusing as we think, but we may need to take off the glasses of some of our traditional interpretations when digging in.

God's descriptions of the end times found in the Old and New Testaments should be carefully and prayerfully examined. Though several items Jesus teaches in his Olivet discourse in Matthew 24–25 and Mark 13 have not yet happened, a number have. The prophet Daniel said that at the time of the end, "the wise shall understand" (Daniel 12:10).[5] Simply put, as these events come closer, the understanding of and dynamic application of Scripture will become clearer to those sincerely seeking wisdom. God reveals clarity to the spiritually wise. This isn't natural wisdom, but the wisdom that comes to a heart set on listening to the Lord, being swayed by him and responding with obedience.

In the summer of 2006, I was with Kelly, our six-month-old son, Noah, and eighty others from around the world on an outreach in several Arab nations. We began in Beirut. Days after arriving, Lebanese Hezbollah fighters kidnapped an Israeli soldier from Lebanon's southern border. Israel responded with a tremendous show of force. Over the next thirty days, a war took place predominantly in Beirut as Israel bombed the homes of known Hezbollah members and sympathizers. Israel destroyed the airport, so supplies from supportive Syria and Iran couldn't get in.

We were staying on the campus of a training seminary in the hills of Beirut, far from the focal point of the bombing. Four days after fighting erupted, we got out by taking a bus to Syria, obtaining a twenty-four-hour transit visa, staying the night in Damascus and traveling on to Amman, Jordan.

Any time Israel is in the news, there is talk among believers of its meaning from an eschatological (study of end times) perspective. At that point, I had not spent time coming to my own Spirit-led conclusions on Israel and its divine role in the end times. Much of what I'd heard seemed rooted more in American culture than in rightly discerning and interpreting the Bible. Our experience in that war zone led me to become a student of the end times. This was not because I wanted to figure out all the dates and specifics of when things would happen, but because the Scriptures on the end times seemed to teach the heart of God, which would give me a clearer understanding of how things would unfold over time, thereby aligning my expectations with truth. How we understand the end times dictates how we live in the present.

NEEDED: DIVINE PERSPECTIVE

The book of Habakkuk sheds light on a primary characteristic message bearers need: divine perspective to rightly interpret what is taking place around us according to God's plans and purposes. We see a divine pattern in this small book. God loves to give divine perspective in the midst of crisis and misunderstanding. It may be that in no other calling than that of a message bearer is that perspective so necessary. Daily occurrences arise that cause questioning and self-doubt. As message bearers periodically face tragedy and pain, discouragements can run rampant.

Habakkuk begins his book confused, questioning God. In the first four verses, his question to God is, "How long will the wicked prosper?" He has been God's prophet to the southern Israelite kingdom of Judah, which has ignored God's words. They're in a backslidden state, and Habakkuk wants to know what God will do about it. God's response in verses 5-11 shocks Habakkuk: justice is coming at the hands of God's own enemies and those of Israel. God will use the dreaded Babylonians to bring justice and to awaken Israel. This is horrifying to Habakkuk. He knows Israel is walking in open compromise against God, but exposing them to the brutality of the Babylonians seems extreme. Aren't the Babylonians more wicked than Israel?

Habakkuk proceeds in verses 12-17 with a clarifying second question: "How can you, the holy God, use them as your instrument of justice?" The whole scenario appears unjust to Habakkuk, perplexing him. He understands Israel's need of punishment, yet he finds it difficult to understand God's use of a people more wicked than Israel to bring this about. Habakkuk wonders how a holy God can accomplish his eternal purposes using an unholy nation.

In confusion, he sets himself on a prayer watch to receive understanding (chapter 2). This was no passive watch. Waiting on God is active; it involves intentionally waiting with zeal and perseverance for God's clarity. Habakkuk models the correct response to God when we don't understand his ways and what he is doing. He isn't offended by God; he is confused and wants divine understanding. His heart is humble, as he is willing to be corrected by God, whom he confesses to be all wise and infinite. God, pleased with the sincerity of his prophet, provides clarity.

God gives Habakkuk a crash course on his ways. The Lord himself is seen as orchestrating the events of Babylon and Israel—not because he has written the covenant people off, but because of his relentless mercy to bring them back to himself. This is a way to understand God as judge—not as a mean God thundering in anger but as a God with a tender heart of love, implementing the least severe means to awaken people to himself. God knows human nature much better than we do and uses this to awaken us to turn to him. God seeks to use judgment to awaken us to how far we have strayed, realigning our hearts so we change our ways. While many respond, many do not.

God doesn't leave his prophet in despair. He agrees with Habakkuk's assessment of Babylon, confirming it will receive harsh judgment itself in the coming days. The book concludes in exuberant certainty in the perfect will and ways of an unseen God. God had met Habakkuk, providing a massive paradigm shift, and Habakkuk worshiped with a heart of gratitude.

The book teaches that being perplexed at circumstances is okay, yet remaining in perplexity is not. God seeks to expand our perspective, replacing it with his own divine perspective. At every stage of life and ministry, we need a broader perspective than before. This is especially true in a complex global environment, in which we easily misinterpret events, potentially missing what God intends to do in and through specific situations.

SEASONS OF LIFE AND MINISTRY

Our lives ebb and flow. We're on a uniquely scripted journey with ups and downs; at times we feel unstoppable and at times we can't get out of bed. The journey has great highs and often devastating lows. Thriving as God's message bearers includes recognizing our spiritual seasons.[6] One reason I value honest biographies is they teach that life isn't easy. Men and women of God go through deep valleys and suffer in various ways. There are no supersaints—only believers obediently taking God at his word.

A misunderstanding of seasons can breed discouragement and even take us out of the race. Examples abound in Scripture and history of those who did not understand a season they were going through. Instead of cooperating with God, discerning each season, they unknowingly stood against him. There are seasons of renewal and seasons in a proverbial wilderness. Seasons of outward fruitfulness and seasons of pruning, when the Lord restricts us. Seasons of answered prayer and seasons of sowing faith-filled intercession with no outward answers. Seasons of God hedging us in and seasons of expansion and growth.

Each season has a divine purpose. We move out of a season according to God's timing when we submit to God's work in us and learn the needed lessons. I've learned to ask God a series of questions in every season: What are you trying to teach me? What do you want me to see that I'm not seeing? How do I need to prepare spiritually to move through this season faithfully? What areas are you maturing in me through this?

Deuteronomy 11:13-14 reveals conditions for experiencing seasons of fruitfulness: "And it shall be that if you earnestly obey My commandments which I command you today, to love the LORD your God and serve Him with all your heart and with all your soul, then I will give you the rain for your land in its season, the early rain and the latter rain, that you may gather in your grain, your new wine, and your oil." Loving and serving God is pivotal to receiving "rain" in its season. When that rain comes, it accomplishes its purpose:

producing spiritual fruit. If we are faithfully loving and serving God (drawing near to him, living in obedience to him, loving his people) from a pure heart in increasing measures, we can expect the rain and then the fruit in time. We resist the temptation to grow weary in loving and serving God.

GUIDANCE AND GOD'S TIMING

Understanding God's timing is important for message bearers. Based on our personality, we're tempted either to move ahead of his timing or to lag behind. Knowing our natural tendency is important. The Lord will undoubtedly orchestrate events to help us grow in trust in his timing.

God's guidance includes a four-faceted principle. We want to discern all four as we step out into the works of God: (1) the specifics of the work he intends us to do (the what), (2) the specifics of the way it's to be undertaken (the how), (3) the timing of its undertaking (the when), and (4) the people we serve with (the who).

During our season in Turkey, Kelly and I sensed God leading us to be involved in training. God provided numerous confirmations over a decade's time. So, we had the "what." The other three dimensions of the training center were unclear. We were not clear on *how* this training would transpire, what the Lord's timing was or who would be involved. Recognizing the lack of these three dimensions, we began to understand that the present time was not God's timing. We needed more clarity in those three areas of guidance, and God has since provided it. Several years later, we're now based in Chiang Mai pursuing the development of a training center.

All four criteria of guidance are essential to realizing God's will. Message bearers often have one or two of the four when they step out in pursuit of a plan. We can endanger ourselves when we move forward without a clearer sense of God's guidance in an undertaking.

We find many scriptural examples of the importance of God's

timing (the when). The Israelites' deliverance from Egypt came exactly as prophesied to Abraham—430 years later. God spoke to Joshua and the Israelites to cross the Jordan at exactly the right time—when the river would be at its lowest. In the book of Judges, God raised up deliverers at exactly the right time—when all seemed lost. Daniel stumbled upon the words of Jeremiah, prophesying the Israelites' seventy-year captivity at exactly the right time. And he realized the seventy years were soon up.

Jesus himself was born in the fullness of time. God knew the exact time in human history to bring forth his Son and serve his purposes. The Macedonian call for Paul included an important element of the timing of God: the Holy Spirit had been preparing that ethnic group for a ready response to the gospel.

God cares about timing in every message bearer's life: the generation we're born in, the people around us in a particular season, the location we are in at a particular time. Each has bearing on his purposes in our generation. Message bearers take steps of great faith at the leading of the Lord, and the timing of each step is essential. Many have taken steps that appeared to be of faith, yet brought devastation on themselves and others. A big factor has been failing to discern God's timing.

The timing lesson is a challenging one, as it requires denying our efforts and ambitions. We surrender impatience, giving God freedom to use us according to his time frame. We surrender our finite understanding and embrace his sovereign plans.

Cooperating with God's timing includes active waiting. The psalms consistently refer to waiting on God. Those who did obtained the promises of God in season, and those who did not got off track. Waiting is a painful process. It leaves us bare before God, in dependence on him. This is precisely what he seeks. This waiting isn't idly biding our time. It's a faith-filled, active process of seeking God for the release of his promises.

10

Persevering with Steadfastness and Stability

Spiritual Key # 9

In our global culture, a neglect of perseverance has caused some fallout. Believers get into ministry roles, but they soon decide the situation wasn't what they expected and end up quitting. At times we do incorrectly interpret God's leading. Yet the sheer volume of such situations is staggering. This points to a defect in the collective character of our generation. We want to produce great ministry but don't want to work hard for it.

A common scenario is a message bearer being led by God and surrendering to serve him. She prepares and finds herself in an unreached ethnic group. Hardships arise. Her team isn't as she'd expected. She thought life as a message bearer would be different. She's lonely, missing loved ones back home. People aren't responding like she'd dreamed. Emotions take over, deceiving her into thinking this isn't what God called her to after all. She rationalizes away her sense of calling and the ways the Lord led her there.

For some, this takes place within the first few months of arriving. God's potential purpose is cut short before it had an opportunity to sprout. For others, it's one, two, three or more years down the road.

It's possible to track such situations to a slowly deteriorating determination to walk in communion with the Lord. When spiritual vitality slips, every other area goes with it.

This doesn't negate the fact that God leads his people to move on sometimes. More often than not, however, ministry commitment is cut short because of a lack of perseverance. The going gets tough, and the grass appears greener elsewhere.

Overcoming difficult situations with perseverance, believing God has led us to a work, develops us in countless other areas of our spiritual lives. Perseverance is an essential spiritual key for thriving as God's message bearers.

LONGEVITY—A KEY TO FRUITFULNESS

A while ago I did an informal study of leaders with fruitful ministries, both historically and in contemporary circles. I was seeking commonalities. Almost 100 percent of the leaders had been in the same ministry for a significant length of time. For many, but not all, that ministry was also in one location. The idea here is that ministry effectiveness doesn't happen overnight. It requires patience over time, waiting on God through disappointments and setbacks, developing a dynamic ministry philosophy, raising up the right people, having a clear, God-inspired vision and more. If we cut this process short by moving into a new ministry role every few years, we generally do not gain the necessary clarity to bear fruit or learn the lessons the Lord intends for us.

Those making the greatest impact do so through persevering in the primary ministry God has called them to. This doesn't mean we don't have many ministry experiences leading up to the revealing of a primary ministry. But once there is a central life work from God, we set ourselves to it with focus. This is our *consecration*. We offer ourselves on God's altar for the work he has ordained, making a commitment to it, come what may. We don't give ourselves back doors to slip out in case the going gets tough. We're in it for the long haul until the Lord clearly shows us something different.

Rick Warren, pastor of Saddleback Church in Lake Forest, California, says he deliberately chose to stay at Saddleback over the past forty years. He says leaders tend to overestimate what they can do in two to three years and underestimate what they can do in twenty to thirty years. He saw the importance of having a cumulative impact in ministry by possessing a long-term view and sticking with it over time.

The history of SVM2 attests to this. We believed in the small role it might be able to play in the work of mobilizing the body of Christ in the Great Commission. Over the past ten years, we have seen it develop and have some influence, but it has not been easy. I've seen the importance of perseverance when circumstances may say otherwise. I've been tempted to quit many times. Each time the Lord reminds me of his guidance, promises and leadership.

Many leaders around the world were watching to see if the work would last, since new mission initiatives are a dime a dozen. The first few years found some supporting the work but taking a "wait and see" stance. Would this initiative stand the test of time? This was especially true among leaders in the Global South, but many are onboard today, because we persevered, not throwing in the towel.

PAUL'S YEARS IN ARABIA

Though we don't like to hear it in our fast-paced world, effective ministries take time to develop. Jesus isn't in a hurry. I'm reminded of Paul. It's often taught that he began preaching immediately after his conversion. Away Paul went as the pioneer missionary, blazing the trail for God's kingdom among the Gentiles. Not even close! Instead, Paul went into the Arabian desert for fourteen long years. The Bible doesn't tell us much about his time there; we simply know it took place (Galatians 2:1).

What was happening during those years of obscurity? Paul was going deep in fellowship with this Jesus revealed on the road to Damascus. They were years of special connection that transformed Paul forever. He received intensive discipleship from Jesus himself and had incredible experiences with God (see, for example, 2 Corinthians 12:4).

Paul had to unlearn most of what he learned under Gamaliel in his Jewish studies. Some of what God showed him, Paul was restricted from discussing. The Spirit unveiled to Paul divine mysteries, deep understandings of his ways, the eternal purpose of the church and the big picture of what God intended to do in the present age and the age to come. When Paul emerged from those years, he possessed divine information no human being had ever received. He emerged as God's tool for opening the Gentile world to the kingdom of God.

Some of us dream of "big ministry" but don't like the idea of God taking much time in preparing us. In the Arabian desert, God was preparing Paul for all he would one day accomplish for the kingdom. Similarly, we're required to go through a desert for the sake of God imparting all that is necessary to pass on to those we serve. Being in a hurry instead of allowing God to impart himself to us as Paul did may be at the root of the body of Christ's weak spiritual state.

CONTENDING FOR EMOTIONAL STABILITY

A key element in cultivating perseverance is emotional stability. Thriving as God's message bearers includes growing in this. Too many of God's people are tossed around, depending on their environment, external circumstances and emotions. We at times fail at being trustworthy. This isn't because we don't want to be reliable. Instead, a character flaw needs to be addressed.

Few of us have brought our emotions under the leadership of Jesus. We change easily, wavering in our emotional state. We do not yet possess a solid and unyielding foundation, a key to developing steadiness in the will of God. A stone is a solid substance—not shaken, blown or easily changed, but firm, strong, unbending, not easily affected by its environment. According to Jesus, the basic foundation of the church is stability—the likeness of a stone. One of the roles of the Holy Spirit is empowering believers to become more emotionally stable over time.

Peter's account provides an encouraging glimpse of the Lord's commitment to empower us with his stability.[1] When Jesus told Peter, "And I also say to you that you are Peter" (Matthew 16:18), he meant, "You are a stone." Peter is a symbol of every disciple, as we all have a role in building God's kingdom globally. We're meant to be stones. Yet, like Peter, not all who are called as stones act like stones—demonstrating courage, strength, perseverance and stability. The promises Jesus gave Peter, saying, "I will give you the keys of the kingdom of heaven," were in operation when Peter was acting "like a stone," which his name means.

It's God who develops stability. We don't cultivate stability and perseverance by trying harder but by allowing him to work in us over time. Initially, Peter was not much of a stone. He was impetuous, shifting with the circumstances around him.[2] He was strong one minute and weak the next. He was firm, then caving. He had to be broken by God over time, just as we do. Our personalities and temperaments will shift until we embrace this ongoing process of breaking.

This is great encouragement! Jesus is committed to overcoming our emotional instability, making us into stones of courage, perseverance and stability.

Two specific situations reveal Peter's proneness to emotional fluctuations. First, within a span of seven verses (Matthew 16:16-23), Peter speaks a divine revelation given by the Father as well as words revealing his lack of understanding. He confesses Jesus as the

Christ, the Son of the living God. Jesus tells him that flesh and blood didn't reveal that, but the Father did. What a wonderful experience for Peter! What he saw was the truth about Jesus' identity and purpose. He was taken to the highest peak of revelation.

Then Jesus tells his disciples of his approaching suffering and death. Peter stands up and rebukes him for such a preposterous thought. Peter was operating in self-will, trusting his own wisdom, forbidding Christ to go and die. He trusted his own thoughts about divine things. The self life was still strong in him, and he fell to the lowest valley.

In the second situation, Jesus tells his disciples of his imminent betrayal and crucifixion, prophesying that even his disciples will run. Peter declares, "Even if all are made to stumble because of you, I will never be made to stumble." This was a sincere statement, but the words came from Peter's emotional self, not from his true self. (See Matthew 26:32-33, 69-75.)

Each of us has done this; we don't know ourselves as well as we think. We're genuine but not familiar with the inner workings of our emotions. Our character isn't as mature as the ease of an emotional moment might lead us to believe. We mean what we say, but when the time comes to back it up, we stumble.

In the first instance, after Jesus tells Peter, "Get behind me, Satan," he proceeds to teach one of his requirements for discipleship: "If anyone desires to come after Me, let him deny himself, and take up his cross, and follow Me" (Matthew 16:24). Jesus told Peter he must deny himself. The self must be ignored, and every attempt it makes to rise must be silenced. Peter didn't understand his true inner self; he thought he was strong and stable in himself. But denying our own strength is a root of true discipleship.[3]

Observe Peter's extreme variances—the difference between his words and actions. First, he told Jesus he would never be caused to stumble, yet he denied him three times. Second, he said he would die with Jesus, yet he trembled with fear at the accusation of a servant girl (Matthew 26:71-72). These incidents paint a picture of how easily Peter was swayed. He changed with the prevailing wind of circumstances, susceptible to his surroundings. His spirit was willing but his flesh was terribly weak, just as ours is.[4] In time, however, Peter developed steadiness. He became what his names means. We will too as we persist in embracing God's stability in us.

A MIND TO SUFFER

An important factor in becoming a stone and having perseverance among the unreached is developing a mind to suffer. First Peter 4:1 states, "Since Christ suffered for us in the flesh, arm yourselves also with the same mind." Being armed with a mind to suffer isn't the same as actually suffering. It's a willingness to endure hardship and trials and a preparation to stand firm if and when such things come. It's a decision made in our hearts despite what we're experiencing. We tell the Lord we're committed to his work, and if this includes facing difficulty, we're willing to do so. This doesn't mean we will suffer, but we will be ready for it. Whether we're currently experiencing hardship or not, we prepare ourselves to suffer.[5] It's the readying of ourselves that the Lord is most interested in.

The following is a common scenario: A message bearer is serving in a nation, and difficulties suddenly arise. He is committed to the work but doesn't yet have a mind to suffer. He hasn't practiced making the choice to be readied for hardship. A helpful test is to ask, "Am I willing to serve the Lord only when situations are good?" Enduring and overcoming hardships is a normal part of ministry. Jesus promised it would be.

Many of us falsely assume that when hardship comes, we will naturally stand firm and persevere. But crisis moments bring out who we truly are. Most often we don't stand firm, because we did not prepare our hearts and minds. Those who prepare aren't shaken when difficulty comes, because they have prepared themselves to endure suffering.

Too many serve the Lord for a time, face trials and unexpected troubles, and quit. The Lord wants to minimize these needless casualties. No matter what comes our way, we commit to persevere faithfully in what he has willed us to do in life and ministry. No matter what problems we face in our environment, in our relationships or in other areas, we press on in faithfulness to the Lord and his calling. We do this out of love for Jesus. He has given us the means to overcome and persevere, so we prepare ourselves daily by deliberately developing a mind to suffer.

CONSIDERING DEPRESSION

Proneness to depression is taking on epidemic proportions in the body of Christ as a whole, and its prevalence among God's message bearers is more common than we may realize. Depression can inhibit perseverance, emotional stability and our ability to cultivate a mind to suffer.

I'm not a psychologist, a psychiatrist or a licensed counselor, so I encourage you to dig deeper into this subject from a psychological/mental perspective.[6] I won't get into a clinical or exhaustive discussion here. I just want to provide a taste of some of the natural, practical and spiritual causes that may play a role in a message bearer's depression.

Depression is a reason many message bearers return home. A few years ago, a research project was undertaken among current and prior message bearers in Turkey with the intent to find out the primary causes of attrition (leaving the mission field). The top reason among a majority of workers was depression. Several mission organizations serving in Turkey said at least one unit (individual or couple) on each team was struggling with mild to severe depression.

It isn't uncommon for message bearers to struggle for long periods with debilitating depression. I'm not referring to "the blues," but to sustained depression not overcome over a period of years. The blues are a normal part of life for all human beings and can be accentuated for message bearers. The difficult situations, isolation and loneliness of serving in another culture often cause periods of discouragement and emotional stress. Pioneer laborers in the mission movement (William Carey, Hudson Taylor, Adoniram Judson and others) themselves experienced periods of deep emotional pain.

Why consider the problem of depression from a mission perspective? First, the goal is to see message bearers thriving in their callings and persevering for the kingdom. Because we know the significance of depression, we must provide help and care to those struggling. Simply surviving isn't the goal. The aim is to enjoy life in the kingdom of God to the fullest. Second, message bearers work to see the kingdom realized and the glory of God known and experienced, but depression makes it difficult to shine the light of Christ in dark places. Those in its clutches want to be free to effectively serve those they are among.

The Bible has so many references to depression that an overview leads to the simple conclusion that depression is common among God's people. From Scripture as well as church and mission history, it's apparent that it has been present among believers since the dawn of time. Psalm 42:5-11 paints a picture of some of the primary issues involved in depression.

> Why are you cast down, O my soul?
> And why are you disquieted within me?
> Hope in God, for I shall yet praise Him
> For the help of His countenance.
> O my God, my soul is cast down within me;

Therefore I will remember You from the land of the Jordan,
And from the heights of Hermon,
From the Hill Mizar.
Deep calls unto deep at the noise of Your waterfalls;
All Your waves and billows have gone over me.
The LORD will command His lovingkindness in the daytime,
And in the night His song shall be with me—
A prayer to the God of my life.
I will say to God my Rock,
"Why have You forgotten me?
Why do I go mourning because of the oppression of
    the enemy?"
As with a breaking of my bones,
My enemies reproach me,
While they say to me all day long,
"Where is your God?"
Why are you cast down, O my soul?
And why are you disquieted within me?
Hope in God;
For I shall yet praise Him,
The help of my countenance and my God.

What are the psalmist's characteristics? The weight of the universe seems to be pressing on him. He is dejected and miserable, troubled, perplexed, worried and anxious. He weeps and is afraid. Worry over his circumstances overwhelms him. His enemies are closing in, speaking lies about him and his God. His emotions are erratic, and his appetite is suppressed.

SOME CAUSES OF DEPRESSION

A new message bearer comes to a country. Maybe he has never struggled with depression. The different language, food, customs and other aspects of the culture leave him exposed to culture stress. He is lonely and feels isolated from his home culture's support systems. Emotional, spiritual and psychological weakness during this phase open him to thinking he made the wrong decision in coming. Left unchecked, these emotions fester, and the message bearer starts to spiral downward into depression. He can't sense the presence of God, seek his face or engage in work. If he continues along this path without finding some relief, he will continue to be depressed.

A person's temperament, personality and emotional makeup can contribute to depression; some temperaments are more prone to depression than others. It's wise for message bearers to know their personality makeup to discern natural tendencies toward depression. Another natural factor is physical condition.[7] This could include a range of physical problems, such as illness or a lack of exercise, which can contribute to a lack of emotional well-being. The spiritual can't be separated from the physical, as human beings are made up of mind, body and spirit. When we're physically not up to par, we're likely to have emotional issues.

Several spiritual factors can make a message bearer susceptible to depression. First is a failure to be grounded in the foundations of our faith. Second is a lack of wholeness or balance in our spiritual lives. Are there unresolved relational issues, such as unforgiveness? Third, are we dwelling too much in our past? Are past failures producing guilt and promoting a sense of helplessness, which can lead to depression? Fourth, is there a propensity toward self-pity? Are things not going the way we thought they would? Is affirmation lacking; are disappointments mounting; are relationships going sour; are we being overlooked?

A fifth spiritual cause may be the most important of all: unhappiness that pulls us into despair. Not knowing how to handle feelings can produce much pain. God created us as emotional beings to experience the deep joy of loving him, the heights of relationships, the power of compassion, the righteous anger against injustice and much more. He has put this feature in the forefront of our beings. Yet we were never meant to live from our feelings, giving them first place. Left to dominate center stage, feelings inevitably bring unhappiness, which can lead to depression.

A helpful way to overcome a tendency to live from feelings is to dictate to our emotions instead of allowing them to dictate to us. The response of the depressed psalmist reveals a key to fighting depression. We speak to ourselves, calling ourselves back to God, fixing our eyes on him. The psalmist called himself to account, speaking to his emotions to come under control. He told himself to gaze on God, and his countenance changed as a result.

Another means of resisting depression is finding contentment. Basic contentment is taught throughout the New Testament and provides a buffer from our tendency to get down on ourselves. We often find believers in less-than-desirable situations choosing to be content and thereby avoiding the power of depression. In Philippians 4:11, Paul teaches the pursuit of contentment no matter the outer circumstances. A few verses later, he writes the much-quoted verse "I can do all things through Christ who strengthens me." Because he was drawing on the empowering life of Christ, no matter what came, Paul could face the situation.

Finally, some depression among message bearers is of another kind entirely. We're in a spiritual battle with a real enemy. Message bearers serve in parts of the world that have been steeped in demonic strongholds for centuries. Intending to further God's kingdom inevitably stirs up a hornet's nest, so we ought to expect and spiritually prepare for a measure of backlash. Satan uses every means to afflict message bearers, and depression can be one of those tools. Serving Jesus in his Great Commission without an adequate theology and some practical experience in spiritual warfare makes us vulnerable.[8] It's necessary to learn how to resist him in such attacks.

11

Pursuing a Focused Life

Spiritual Key # 10

Thriving as God's effective message bearer includes an awareness of how he has created us and then zeroing in on his vision for us. We know intellectually that God has a plan for our lives. Most often, however, we don't feel connected to that plan in our day-to-day lives and don't feel we're moving forward in it. God wants us confident in his unfolding plan as we serve him—a plan that has been in existence since the foundation of the world. Seeing it come to fruition takes patience, commitment and tenacity. This includes cultivating a growing sense of God's leading and making deliberate daily choices to walk through life and ministry with focus.

PLEASING GOD

Pleasing God is one goal in pursuing a focused life. This ambition is meant to motivate us. A message bearer's purpose is to be faithful and obedient as she orders her life around the vision of pleasing God in every sphere of her life and ministry. We do not live to be known, to receive affirming pats on the back or to obtain happiness or financial kickbacks. We live to move the heart of God through focusing our lives on the high goal of pleasing him in all we do. Becoming students of what pleases God results in knowing God better—his ways, his thoughts, his will and his purposes. Seeking to please God first and foremost results in a greater grasp on how to live for his glory.

CULTIVATING TRUE VISION

There is a lot of talk these days about *vision*. It has become a buzzword—even a cliché. True vision isn't merely a set of good ideas or action steps. It's listening to God's voice, discerning the what, how and when of his will, seeking to please him and determining to respond in unwavering faith (though we may waver at times). True vision grows over time as we faithfully respond to the Lord's leading. It's tested as we go through a death of that very vision, and God resurrects it in his timing. God is jealous for his glory, and true vision is realized, not according to human capacities, but by his initiation and involvement. True vision is actualized through a life that becomes increasingly more focused. Such a person is developing habits to carry the vision God is unfolding.

Message bearers often have little focus because we have not clarified, with God, the purpose of our life. All believers have general purpose: to deepen our love for God, to obey his Word and the leading of the Spirit within, to pursue justice in all realms, to serve others and to live with humility. A problem often arises when we seek to discern the specific, individual destiny we each possess in God. We may have vague ideas, but we have not identified them clearly enough to help us in attaining a focused life.

WHAT IS A FOCUSED LIFE?

A focused life is a life moving toward the following four-fold emphasis:

1. Living a life dedicated exclusively to carrying out God's unique purposes for it

2. Identifying the focal issues of life purpose, major role, effective methodology and ultimate contribution

3. Allowing an increasing prioritization of activities around the focal points

4. Seeing results in a satisfying life of being and doing[1]

Some common elements have been identified among message bearers who are focused:

1. Long-term ministries in a role that fits the individual

2. A lifelong involvement in serving Christ to fulfill a specific destiny

3. A concentration on achieving certain important goals, leaving behind legacies for the ongoing work of Christ

4. A focus on the Word of God for personal growth and ministry

5. The shaping work of God to move toward focus, which teaches crucial lessons[2]

A LIFE-PURPOSE STATEMENT

Those who are increasingly used by God have some form of what is commonly called a life-purpose statement. A life purpose is a burden, a calling, a task or a driving force that motivates a believer to fulfill something or see something done.[3] It involves underlying motivations that energize the message bearer in his spiritual life and ministry. It is reflected in the varying tasks and goals to which the message bearer is committed.[4]

A life purpose unfolds over a lifetime, and it isn't always apparent initially. The following decade-by-decade process is common for a message bearer who came to genuine faith in Jesus in her teens. Usually in her twenties to thirties, she makes a commitment to serve God. Character development and the seed of her life purpose are evident. In her thirties and forties, her basic life purpose firms up. In her forties and fifties, that life purpose is clarified, modified and expanded, and additional pieces of the purpose might be added to it. Message bearers make decisions about life and ministry based on their understanding of who God has made them to be and the purpose he is shaping them for. These decisions lead to full, effective, purposeful lives, which others acknowledge to be a focused life.[5]

A life-purpose statement is a few paragraphs detailing what we believe God has mandated in our life and ministry. It highlights life and ministry goals, and it focuses on ongoing development toward those goals. It's a fluid document, ever changing as the Lord teaches, leads, guides and clarifies. By faith, we lay out in writing and in broad strokes the focal points God has already revealed to us. As time goes on, God provides more detail, bringing more focus to particular points. We will not grasp the "how" of these things all at once.

A life-purpose statement usually focuses on three different components of our life:

1. A focus on our inner life, primarily on what we are becoming in our relationship with Christ. What do we want Jesus to say about us related to our depth of communion and experiential knowledge of him when we stand before him? What are our goals related to spiritual disciplines and our mastery of the Bible? What are major areas of inner-life development we want to mature in?

2. A focus on family and relationships. Our family and relationships are important to us. We don't want a life of "doing" in ministry at the expense of the health of relationships. They come first.

3. A focus on what we believe God has gifted and ordained us to be about in serving him. We write out what God has already revealed to us about how he might want to use us for his glory.

I first jotted down such thoughts when I was twenty-two. At that time, my whole life-purpose statement was only a few sentences long. What you see below is a version that evolved over the past seventeen years. I'm not necessarily doing all these things, but they are what I believe (at this point) God has mandated me to be about. I hope this example will help you write your own statement according to the calling God has uniquely scripted for you.

I purpose to be a man after God's own heart; a surrendered bondservant of my master, daily submitting my time, energies, finances and other resources to the Lord for his pleasure; finding my identity as a lover of God and one who is the beloved of God and never in a role or position or other worldly marker; marked by the powerful presence of the most high God; continuously conformed to the likeness of Christ Jesus, my king; abiding consistently in him; yielded to the Holy Spirit and daily receiving his fullness; possessing a vibrant, victorious and ever-expanding prayer life; saturated with his holy Word, studying it, meditating on it and mastering it over a lifetime; living by faith in spheres of life and proving the faithfulness of God time and time again; functioning with spiritual perspective and overcoming spiritual and natural giants; receiving the effective training of God to walk in the destiny he has ordained for me.

I purpose to be a friend to my family, serving Kelly as Christ serves the church, cherishing her and leading her as our great bridegroom leads us; seeking Jesus together, making our home an altar dedicated to the worship and devotion of God; serving my children, Noah and Emma, and teaching them the ways of God the nature of God and the greatness of God that they may be spiritually prepared to face ever-increasing darkness through encountering God's glory.

I purpose to be a prophet to the nations, devoted to equipping, training and exhorting the body of Christ globally to abandoned devotion to Christ Jesus, and our divine mandate of proclaiming the gospel of the kingdom among the forgotten in these last days; effectively stewarding the gifts of vision, exhortation, apostolic ministry and faith in leadership to serve the global cooperative mission movement; walking in networking power, according to God's enabling, to accomplish this; utilizing the written word to communicate and influence through a writing ministry; growing consistently in the use of the gifts of the Spirit and functioning as a unifier and bridge among the charismatic and evangelical realms of Christ's body; pursuing faithfulness and obedience in the face of pressures, setbacks and disappointments.

Here are some important ideas to remember as you prepare a life-purpose statement:

- What destiny experiences have I had over my lifetime, and what has God led me to be about as a result?

- What are the highlights of both my inner life of "being" with God and my "doing" in ministry?

- It isn't a wish list but a statement at this time of what you believe God wants to do in and through you.

- It is based on God's dealings in your life, affirmations from others, inner peace, prophetic direction and so on.[6]

CLARIFYING OUR LIFE PURPOSE

God has special ways of helping us clarify and understand our life purpose. One means is destiny experiences, which are special interventions (sometimes a series over time) through which God provides a major emphasis that flows through a message bearer's life and often gives strategic direction. These are benchmarks through which God reveals something important for ongoing growth and development.[7] Over a lifetime, a message bearer attuned to the leading of God will generally recognize four to eight such crucial experiences. These are anchors we hold as we progress in serving God.

An example is Joseph's two dreams at the age of seventeen (Genesis 37:5-10). These were a destiny experience, as they ignited a sense of purpose in his young life. He knew the dreams were from God and signified a specific purpose for him. Joseph could not, however, have imagined their meaning at seventeen. Over the next twenty-two years, he clung to those dreams through thick and thin. They were finally realized when he was thirty-nine. The key was that Joseph remembered them, believed in them and clung to God to see them realized in due time.

The human mind can't always remember events—even positive ones. Recording our experiences with God helps us remember. God can use this record years into the future. We look back and are reminded of something he did or said that directly speaks to something we face right now, and encouragement and confidence fill us. If journaling doesn't fit your personality, consider blogging, photographing key moments or making crafts that symbolize key markers from God.

Kelly and I have a journal of specific ways God has intervened and guided us over the past fifteen years. I can honestly say that without such a record of how God has revealed himself, we would be in a very different place right now. This has primarily occurred as we look back and see the cumulative leading and promises of God. Without this record we would have been tempted to go in very different directions.

WHAT TYPE OF MESSAGE BEARER AM I?

It's essential to clarify what type of message bearer God has created you to be, because this will help you be more focused. There are at least three primary types of message bearers. These types have less to do with specific ministries and more to do with the way God has created each of us (personality, temperament, critical-thinking capacity, problem-solving capacity, decision making and so on) and what spiritual gifts he has given us. Countless message bearers fail to discern which type they are and end up serving in a capacity they aren't wired for. They work hard, applying themselves, yet are frustrated and discouraged.

There are many more subcategories fitting under these broad types, but we will stick with the primary three here. They aren't in any order of importance, as all three are essential for the fulfillment of the Great Commission.

1. Serving the Great Commission through support ministries. These include works of administration, accounting, teaching message bearers' children, IT, event planning and a multitude of other helps needed to keep ministries moving forward. These helpers do not stay in their home country, however. They're crucial on the field, working alongside frontline church planters and others working with a growing indigenous church.

2. Serving growing indigenous believers. These come alongside local believers with training, mentoring, modeling, teaching, intercession and so on. They usually thrive in structured environments. They do best coming into a situation already in place. They do not necessarily plant the churches but serve them by developing leaders, imparting principles for effective discipleship and helping instill a vision for proactive outreach and crosscultural ministry.

3. Serving as frontline church planters. These are usually visionaries with pioneering spirits. They don't need a lot of structure in place, as they create structure on their own. They're comfortable with ambiguity and a vague role description. They're

drawn to places where the true church of Christ does not exist. They're wired for effectiveness in such scenarios and usually have gifts of evangelism, apostleship, teaching and perseverance, sprinkled with gifts of faith and miracles. Once indigenous churches are developed, they seek to move on to another unreached area.

A friend of mine was a frontline church planter among the unreached. He had sensed God calling him as a message bearer when he was in college, and he had assumed church planting was the only way to do that. Over time he became frustrated in his work and thought something was wrong with him. This went on for months. Finally, a leader in his mission agency recognized something was wrong. Through prayer and dialogue, they realized he was not called as a church planter. He began teaching message bearers' children at a school and found his gifts and strengths well utilized. He was definitely called to serve the Great Commission but needed to find his niche. He has now been teaching at an international mission school for many years—and he is thriving.

A TIME MANAGEMENT PLAN FOR REMAINING FOCUSED

There are 168 hours in a week, 672 hours in a month and 8,064 hours in a year. These hours are at the disposal of every person equally. A way to please the Lord is to guard these hours, using them to move toward the life purpose he has intended for us. If we fail to use time well, someone or something else will seize it for other purposes.

The discipline of time management isn't innate. In fact, it's the opposite. Left to ourselves, most of us waste vast amounts of time. Without an increasingly clear vision of God's purpose for our lives, we will most likely fail to use time in the right way. However, message bearers are generally not taught how to manage time. From our early years, others have managed our time. This extended even into college, when we were told what time our classes were. We may still be told when to go to our jobs and when to leave, what meetings we're required to be at and so on.

Being a message bearer usually means directing our own time without someone looking over our shoulder. This can be a problem for new message bearers, who are thrust into managing their own time but don't have the skills for doing so. Thriving as God's message bearer means taking hold of time and carefully managing it, focusing our life and ministry on what God has called us to do.

One of the greatest enemies of effectively using time is the "tyranny of the urgent."[8] Urgent issues rise to the top of our priority list, but focusing on them can keep us from doing what's most important. Urgent issues are different from common interruptions at work and from emergencies. The tyranny of the urgent keeps believers consumed with issues that have no spiritual impact. But how do we combat this? An important step is to develop a time management plan. This can help us take control of the hours we are given to further the work God seeks to do in and through us. The entire plan is meant to serve our overall life purpose and to help us progress toward it.

Not all personality types or cultures find a time management plan helpful. Some find it better to break up their schedules not by time but by relationships. The point is not the particular model but taking hold of our schedules and progressing faithfully toward God's focus in and through our lives.

With that said, I present a time-oriented structure I've found helpful. There are different ways to divide up our allotted weekly 168 hours. I encourage breaking it into one-hour intervals. This means we want each one-hour period of each twenty-four-hour period to serve the overall life purpose God has given us. We divide our lives into categories of activity that are part of natural life and that move us toward our destiny in God. We ask helpful questions to determine what these categories are, keeping in mind our commitment to move faithfully toward our life purpose.

The following list of categories is a useful starting point. These aren't in a particular order.

- *Family.* Specific ways and time allotments necessary to nurture our marriage (if we're married) and spend quality time with our family (if we have children). We write into the schedule specific ways we will do this.

- *Relationships.* Specific days and times when we will cultivate meaningful relationships the Lord has given us. This includes fellowship with couples or individuals as well as other families, and so on.

- *Ministry.* We plan our time to serve those the Lord has entrusted to us or the specific work he has led us to at that time.

- *Language learning.* Learning the language as soon as possible is a priority for new message bearers. This takes lots of time and focused energy. It isn't a small undertaking and needs to be planned for on a day-by-day basis.

- *Money (giving and saving).* What are the financial resources God has given to us, and what is he calling us to do with those resources? How much of it will we give and how much will we save, and when? These are important questions often left to chance or emotions.

- *Bible study.* What part of the day will we give to going deep in God's Word? We want to increase this amount as often as possible because being students of God's Word is key to being equipped as thriving message bearers.

- *Prayer.* If we do not plan a time and location to seek God's face, it will all too easily not happen. It needs to be included in our daily, weekly and monthly schedules.

- *Fasting.* What meals or entire days in any given week or month will we give to fasting from food? Seek to be consistent in fasting one meal or one day a week.

- *Leisure.* It's important to be rejuvenated by hobbies and other leisure activities that build us up. Write them into your schedule and make time for them.

- *Rest.* Consider the number of hours of sleep you need each night to function adequately. Don't indulge in more sleep than necessary, and don't cut yourself short on needed sleep either. Most people need seven to nine hours of sleep per night (yet this can differ from culture to culture).

- *Exercise.* Keeping our bodies in shape by eating right and exercising is important to our calling.

- *Serving.* Often we get so involved in our ministry that it becomes self-serving, and we forget the calling to simply serve. When are times we can serve another's work or serve in a capacity outside of our specific ministry?

- *Personal development.* Pursuing our mandate from God means always developing our inner lives and ministry capacities. Plan for how and when you will read books, listen to messages or engage in personal growth projects.

- *Ongoing training.* There may be a need to get further training, and the Lord might lead you to engage part time in that. This might include training from a formal institution or through workshops, conferences or courses. A purposeful mentoring relationship can also fall under the category of training.

We take these categories (and others that are particular to each of us) and allot daily, weekly and monthly time intervals to them. We print off a weekly calendar and prayerfully write out what we want to do, when and for how long. We want to be able to say what we're doing on specific days and times for the next three months, six months and so on to maintain our focus on our purpose in God. It's important to tweak our time management plan here and there every few months to make sure it's working for us and, most importantly, to make sure we're working toward our goals.

Don't expect to keep to your schedule 100 percent of the time. At 80 percent of the time, you're doing extremely well. Keep focused, but don't forget to give yourself grace.

Epilogue

In this book we've considered essential spiritual keys for thriving as God's message bearers. If taken to heart, these keys help to equip the body of Christ as we progress in our calling toward the fulfillment of the Great Commission. If you're a message bearer, I pray God uses these encouragements to set you on a course of being continually equipped to serve the unreached and unengaged. May you not just hear these things but commit yourself to be a doer of them. If you're a mission agency leader, I trust God will use these concepts to enable your agency to empower message bearers to be prepared to succeed at the highest level. If you're a local church leader or in campus ministry, my prayer is you will be able to use these principles to set the bar as high as possible as you engage future message bearers among the unreached and unengaged.

The work of seeing the gospel planted among every unreached and unengaged ethnic group is difficult—even impossible—when done in our own strength. However, as we align with Jesus' kingdom ways of building his global body, this reality could be realized in our lifetime. The fulfillment of the Great Commission isn't some far-off goal, but this doesn't minimize the severity of the call; the most resistant, hostile ethnic groups are those left to reach, and the enemy will not give up ground easily. But if a new generation of God's message bearers is raised up and functions according to many of the spiritual keys highlighted in this book, we could make considerable headway.

"The fulfillment of the Great Commission" isn't a pep-rally slogan but a call for the global church to return to its reason for existence. It's a call to mobilize the whole body to take up its role in this great purpose and to send and support the best and brightest from our local ministries as crosscultural message bearers to the unreached and unengaged. We do so by teaching them to cultivate the essential spiritual keys found in this book, as well as many others. We're moved with a sense of urgency, not with a task mindset but out of a heart of obedience to Jesus as he has commanded us to make his Great Commission the centerpiece of our ministry as the body of Christ.

Acknowledgments

Many thanks to message bearers around the world from multitudes of national backgrounds that I've learned from over the years. You are my heroes! As I wrote, many of you were the standard for spiritual equipping I kept in mind.

I'm indebted to the SVM2 staff team in Chiang Mai, Thailand, as they picked up slack on many projects while I dedicated time to putting this book together. Specifically, I thank my wife, Kelly, who is an embodiment of the ten spiritual keys this book contains.

I'm inspired by pastors, leaders and teachers who maintain a high standard of what it means to follow Christ in a dark world. May we never lower Jesus' standards based on our own inadequacies but trumpet his terms above all else.

Special thanks to Jeanette Littleton for early editing suggestions and help on the manuscript, and Jane Rumph for editorial consulting expertise all along the way.

Finally, thanks to the editorial staff at InterVarsity Press for believing in the concept and making this book a reality. Senior editor Al Hsu has been a joy to work with, doing so from across continents and time zones. InterVarsity Press's commitment to excellence and professionalism is second to none.

Notes

FOREWORD

[1]Dallas Willard, *The Great Omission: Rediscovering Jesus' Essential Teachings on Discipleship* (Oxford: Monarch Books, 2006).

INTRODUCTION: SETTING THE STAGE

[1]See the Joshua Project website: www.joshuaproject.net.

[2]Kurt Miller, "Definition of an Unreached People Group," *The Church Planter Blog*, March 7, 2007, http://thechurchplanter.blogspot.com/2007/03/definition-of-unreached-people-group.html.

[3]For a listing of these people groups, see Finishing the Task, "People Group List," www.finishingthetask.com.

[4]See SVM2's website for more information: www.SVM2.net.

[5]William Taylor, *Too Valuable to Lose: Exploring the Causes and Cures of Missionary Attrition* (Pasadena, CA: William Carey Library, 1997), p. 89.

[6]See the following book list for helpful books on general missiological, strategy and language-learning principles: William Taylor, ed., *Global Missiology for the 21st Century* (Grand Rapids: Baker Academic, 2000); Andrew Walls and Cathy Ross, *Mission in the 21st Century* (Maryknoll, NY: Orbis, 2008); Paul G. Hiebert, *Anthropological Insights for Missionaries* (Grand Rapids: Baker Books, 1985); David Garrison, *Church Planting Movement: How God Is Redeeming a Lost World* (Midlothian, VA: Wigtake Resources, 2012); Jerry Trousdale, *Miraculous Movements: How Hundreds of Thousands of Muslims Are Falling in Love with Jesus* (Nashville: Thomas Nelson, 2012); Thomas and Betty Sue Brewster, *Language Acquisition Made Practical: Field Methods for Language Learners* (Pasadena, CA: Lingua House, 1976).

CHAPTER 1: WHAT IS THE SPIRIT SAYING?

[1]Andrew Murray, *The Key to the Missionary Problem* (Chatsworth, CA: Christian Literature Crusade, 1981), p. 131.

[2]Rick Joyner, *The Harvest* (Fort Mill, SC: Morningstar Publications, 2007), p. 17.

[3]*Self life* is a concept dealt with in Roy Hession's book *The Calvary Road* (Chatsworth, CA: Christian Literature Crusade, 1980). The self life includes all that springs from "self," which is sin. It includes complacency, self-pity, self-seeking, self-indulgence, sensitiveness, touchiness, resentment, self-defense, insecurity, self-consciousness, worry, fear, unbelief and more.

[4]Bonnie Harvey, *D. L. Moody—An American Evangelist* (Colorado Springs: Authentic, 2008), p. 7.

[5]John Walvoord, *The Millennial Kingdom* (Grand Rapids: Zondervan, 1959), p. 278.

CHAPTER 2: SPIRITUAL KEY # 1: BEING SATURATED WITH THE POWERFUL PRESENCE OF GOD

[1]A. T. Pierson, *George Müller of Bristol* (Eugene, OR: Kregel Publications, 1999), p. 15.

[2]J. Robert Clinton, *Titus: Apostolic Ministry* (Altadena, CA: Barnabas Publishers, 2001), p. 154.

[3]Andrew Murray, *Absolute Surrender* (Springdale, PA: Whitaker House, 1981), p. 89.

[4]Ruth A. Tucker, *From Jerusalem to Irian Jaya* (Grand Rapids: Zondervan, 1983), pp. 90-93. Also, Brainerd's journal and biography, published by Jonathan Edwards, have had a tremendous impact on the modern mission movement. I've read his journals several times and each time find renewed spiritual energy to seek God's fullness in and through my life: Jonathan Edwards, *The Life and Diary of David Brainerd* (Peabody, MA: Hendrickson Publications, 2006).

[5]Tucker, *From Jerusalem*, pp. 158-63.

[6]Ibid.

[7]J. Robert Clinton, *Nehemiah Clinton Leadership Commentary* (Altadena, CA: Barnabas Publishers, 2002), p. 123.

[8]Loren Cunningham, *Is That Really You, God?* (Seattle: YWAM Publishing, 1984).

[9]C. Howard Hopkins, *John R. Mott: A Biography* (Grand Rapids: Eerdmans, 1980); Mr. and Mrs. Howard Taylor, *Hudson Taylor's Spiritual Secret* (Chicago: Moody Press, 1984); David McCasland, *Oswald Chambers: Abandoned to God* (Grand Rapids: Discovery House, 1983); W. M. Douglas, *Andrew Murray and His Message* (Grand Rapids: Baker, 1981); Timothy Tow, *John Sung: My Teacher* (Singapore: Christian Life Publishers, 1985); Basil Miller, *Praying Hyde: A Man of Prayer* (Grand Rapids: Zondervan, 1943); John Weinlick, *Count Zinzendorf* (Bethlehem, PA: The Moravian Church in America, 1984).

[10]Jim Cromarty, *It Is Not Death to Die: A New Biography of Hudson Taylor* (Fearn, UK: Christian Focus Publications, 2008), p. 7.

[11]For more information, see Brother Lawrence, *Practicing the Presence of God* (New Kensington, PA: Whitaker House, 1982).

CHAPTER 3: SPIRITUAL KEY # 2: EMBRACING HUMILITY

[1]Andrew Murray, *Humility* (Springdale, PA: Whitaker House, 1982), p. 21.

[2]Roy Hession, *The Calvary Road* (Fort Washington, PA: CLC, 1990), p. 22.

[3]See the following list for helpful books focusing on Jesus' humility through the cross: John Owen, *The Glory of Christ* (Carlisle, PA: Banner of Truth Trust, 2000); John Piper, *Fifty Reasons Why Jesus Came to Die* (Wheaton, IL: Crossway Books, 2006); John Piper, *The Passion of Jesus Christ* (Wheaton, IL: Crossway Books, 2004); John Stott, *The Cross of Christ* (Downers Grove, IL: InterVarsity Press, 1986); Henrietta Mears, *What Jesus Is All About* (Ventura, CA: Regal, 2004).

[4]Murray, *Humility*, p. 23.

[5]Andrew Murray, *Absolute Surrender* (Springdale, PA: Whitaker House, 1981), p. 62.

[6]Mabel Williamson, *Have We No Rights?* (Chicago: Moody Press, 1957), p. 5.

[7]For more information, read John Pollock, *The Cambridge Seven* (Great Britain: Christian Focus Publications, 2006).

CHAPTER 4: SPIRITUAL KEY # 3: HUNGERING AND THIRSTING FOR GOD

[1]Ryan Shaw, *Engaging the Holy Spirit: Understanding His Dynamics Toward the Fulfillment of the Great Commission* (Armstrong, MO: IGNITE Media, 2012), p. 41.

[2]The following is a link to a PDF full of truths to speak over ourselves,

titled "Who I Am in Christ": www.prayertoday.org/2004/PDF/Guides/ Who-I-Am.PDF.

[3]Mike Bickle, *After God's Own Heart* (Lake Mary, FL: Charisma House, 2009), p. 45.

CHAPTER 5: SPIRITUAL KEY # 4: BEING CLOTHED WITH GOD'S WORD

[1]J. Robert Clinton, *Clinton's Biblical Leadership Commentary* (Altadena, CA: Barnabas Publishers, 1999), p. 325.

[2]Ibid.

[3]A. T. Pierson, *George Müller of Bristol* (Eugene, OR: Kregel Publications, 1999), p. 138.

[4]See the following list for helpful books giving Bible overviews and other study helps: J. Sidlow Baxter, *Explore the Book: A Survey and Study of Each Book from Genesis to Revelation* (Grand Rapids: Zondervan, 1960); G. Campbell Morgan, *An Exposition of the Whole Bible* (Westwood, NJ: Revell, n.d.); G. Campbell Morgan, *Life Applications from Every Chapter of the Bible* (Grand Rapids: Revell, 1926); Henrietta Mears, *What the Bible Is All About* (Ventura, CA: Regal, 1983); David Pawson, *Unlocking the Bible: A Unique Overview of the Whole Bible* (London: HarperCollins, 2007); Gordon Fee, *How to Read the Bible for All Its Worth* (Grand Rapids: Zondervan, 2003); Howard Vos, *Effective Bible Study: A Guide to Sixteen Methods* (Grand Rapids: Zondervan, 1956).

CHAPTER 6: SPIRITUAL KEY # 5: DISCERNING GOD'S GUIDANCE AND REVELATION

[1]Richard Clinton, *Starting Well* (Altadena, CA: Barnabas Publishers, 1998), p. 80.

[2]Ibid., p. 81.

[3]Ibid., p. 85.

[4]See the following list for helpful books for practically growing in hearing God's voice: Dallas Willard, *Hearing God: Developing a Conversational Relationship with God* (Downers Grove, IL: InterVarsity Press, 2012); Henry and Richard Blackaby, *Hearing God's Voice* (Nashville: B&H Books, 2002); Mary Ruth Swope, *Hearing from God* (Springdale, PA: Whitaker House, 1987).

[5]Dick Eastman, *Change the World School of Prayer Manual* (Colorado Springs: Every Home for Christ International, 1991), pp. 159-67.

⁶Rick Joyner, *The Prophetic Ministry* (Fort Mill, SC: Morningstar Publications, 2008), p. 91.

⁷See the following list for helpful books for growing in understanding spiritual gifts and specifically prophecy: Jack Deere, *The Beginner's Guide to the Gift of Prophecy* (Ann Arbor, MI: Vine Books, 2001); Dr. Bill Hamon, *Prophets and Personal Prophecy* (Shippensburg, PA: Destiny Image, 1987); Mike Bickle, *Growing in the Prophetic* (Lake Mary, FL: Charisma House, 2008); J. Oswald Sanders, *The Holy Spirit and His Gifts* (Grand Rapids: Zondervan, 1940).

CHAPTER 7: SPIRITUAL KEY # 6: PURSUING A LIFESTYLE OF PRAYER

¹Andrew Murray, *Key to the Missionary Problem* (Chatsworth, CA: Christian Literature Crusade, 1981), p. 153.

²J. Robert Clinton, *The Joshua Portrait* (Altadena, CA: Barnabas Publishers, 1990), p. 31.

³E. M. Bounds, *The Complete Works of E. M. Bounds on Prayer* (Peabody, MA: Prince Press, 2000), p. 464.

⁴Handley Moule, *Charles Simeon: Pastor of a Generation* (UK: Christian Focus Publications, 1997), p. 67.

⁵John Wesley, *The Journal of John Wesley: A Selection* (Oxford: Oxford University Press, 1987), p. 121.

⁶Andrew Bonar, *The Life of Robert Murray M'Cheyne* (Carlisle, PA: Banner of Truth Trust, 1990), p. 67.

⁷Bounds, *The Complete Works*, p. 464.

⁸Courtney Anderson, *To the Golden Shore: The Life of Adoniram Judson* (Valley Forge, PA: Judson Press, 1987), p. 465.

⁹Bounds, *The Complete Works*, pp. 460-70.

¹⁰See the following list for helpful books about fasting and prayer: James Lee Beall, *The Adventure of Fasting: A Practical Guide* (Old Tappan, NJ: Revell, 1974); Derek Prince, *Shaping History Through Prayer and Fasting* (Old Tappan, NJ: Revell, 1973); Bill Bright, *The Transforming Power of Fasting and Prayer* (Orlando, FL: New Life Publications, 1997); Ronnie Floyd, *The Power of Prayer and Fasting* (Nashville: B&H, 1997); Arthur Wallis, *God's Chosen Fast* (Fort Washington, PA: Christian Literature Company, 1997).

¹¹Franklin Hall, *The Fasting Prayer* (Phoenix, AZ: self-published, 1947), p. 10.

[12]Mike Bickle, *After God's Own Heart* (Lake Mary, FL: Charisma House, 2004), p. 128.

[13]See the following list for helpful books concerning historic revival and how God moves: Mark Shaw, *Global Awakening: How 20th-Century Revivals Triggered a Christian Revolution* (Downers Grove, IL: InterVarsity Press, 2010); Leonard Ravenhill, *Why Revival Tarries* (Minneapolis: Bethany House, 1991); J. Edwin Orr, *The Second Great Awakening in Britain* (London: Marshall, Morgan and Scott, 1953); Jonathan Edwards, *Jonathan Edwards on Revival* (Carlisle, PA: Banner of Truth Trust, 1958); Richard Riss, *A Survey of 20th-Century Revival Movements in North America* (Peabody, MA: Hendrickson Publishers, 1988); J. Edwin Orr, *The Flaming Tongue: The Impact of 20th-Century Revivals* (Chicago: Moody Press, 1973).

[14]See the following list for helpful books on intercessory prayer: Andrew Murray, *With Christ in the School of Prayer* (Springdale, PA: Whitaker House, 1981); Andrew Murray, *The Ministry of Intercession* (Springdale, PA: Revell, 1964); Dutch Sheets, *Intercessory Prayer* (Ventura, CA: Regal, 1996); E. M. Bounds, *E. M. Bounds on Prayer* (Springdale, PA: Whitaker House, 1997).

[15]W. M. Douglas, *Andrew Murray and His Message* (New York: Revell, [1930s]), p. 273.

[16]*The Journal of John Wesley: A Selection*, ed. Elisabeth Jay (Oxford: Oxford University Press, 1987), p. 47.

[17]John Weinlick, *Count Zinzendorf* (Bethlehem, PA: The Moravian Church of America, 1984), p. 79.

[18]Ibid., p. 113.

[19]Andrew Murray, *Key to the Missionary Problem* (Chatsworth, CA: Christian Literature Crusade, 1981), p. 48.

[20]Arthur Wallis, *God's Chosen Fast* (Fort Washington, PA: CLC, 1997), p. 56.

[21]A. T. Pierson, *George Müller of Bristol* (Grand Rapids: Kregel Books, 1999), p. 170.

[22]It is helpful to pray Paul's and Peter's apostolic prayers for believers and ministries. Look in the Epistles for the prayers these leaders pray over the churches and pray likewise over believers globally.

[23]Mike Bickle, *After God's Own Heart* (Lake Mary, FL: Charisma House, 2004), p. 139.

CHAPTER 8: SPIRITUAL KEY # 7: COOPERATING WITH GOD'S TWOFOLD PURPOSE

[1]See the following books for further understanding of growing in holiness: J. C. Ryle, *Holiness* (Durham, UK: Evangelical Press, 1979); Floyd Mc-Clung, *Holiness and the Spirit of the Age* (Eugene, OR: Harvest House, 1990); Jerry Bridges, *The Pursuit of Holiness* (Colorado Springs: NavPress, 2006).

[2]Andrew Murray, *Humility* (Springdale, PA: Whitaker House, 1982), p. 69.

[3]See the following for helpful books concerning the kingdom of God: George Eldon Ladd, *The Gospel of the Kingdom: Scriptural Studies in the Kingdom of God* (Grand Rapids: Eerdmans, 1959); E. Stanley Jones, *The Unshakable Kingdom and the Unchanging Person* (Bellingham, WA: McNett Press, 1995); Arthur Glasser, *Kingdom and Mission* (Pasadena, CA: Fuller Seminary Press, 1989).

[4]George Eldon Ladd, *A Commentary on the Revelation of John* (Grand Rapids: Eerdmans, 1972), p. 82.

[5]Andrew Murray, *Raising Your Children for Christ* (New Kensington, PA: Whitaker House, 1984), p. 168.

[6]John Piper, *Filling Up the Afflictions of Christ* (Wheaton, IL: Crossway Books, 2009), p. 15.

[7]Roland Allen, *Missionary Methods: St. Paul's or Ours?* (Grand Rapids: Eerdmans, 1962), p. 68.

CHAPTER 9: SPIRITUAL KEY # 8: UNDERSTANDING THE TIMES AND SEASONS OF GOD

[1]See, for example, Rick Dunn and Jana Sundene, *Shaping the Journey of Emerging Adults* (Downers Grove, IL: InterVarsity Press, 2012).

[2]See Kevin Belmonte, *Hero for Humanity: A Biography of William Wilberforce* (Colorado Springs: NavPress, 2002).

[3]See Ferdinand Schlingensiepen, *Dietrich Bonhoeffer: Martyr, Thinker, Man of Resistance* (London: T&T Clark, 2012).

[4]See the following list for helpful books on the end times: David Pawson, *When Jesus Returns* (London: Hodder & Stoughton, 1995); George Eldon Ladd, *The Last Things* (Grand Rapids: Eerdmans, 1978); George Eldon Ladd, *The Blessed Hope* (Grand Rapids: Eerdmans, 1956).

[5]J. C. Ryle, *Are You Ready for the End of Time?* (Fearn, UK: Christian Focus Publications, 2001), p. 106.

[6]See Bruce Demarest, *Seasons of the Soul: Stages of Spiritual Development* (Downers Grove, IL: InterVarsity Press, 2009).

CHAPTER 10: SPIRITUAL KEY # 9: PERSEVERING WITH STEADFASTNESS AND STABILITY

[1]Watchman Nee, *The Character of God's Workman* (New York: Christian Fellowship Publishers, 1988), p. 127.

[2]Ibid., p. 128.

[3]Andrew Murray, *Absolute Surrender* (Springdale, PA: Whitaker House, 1981), p. 58.

[4]Ibid., p. 130.

[5]Nee, *Character*, p. 37.

[6]See these books and articles for further information on depression: Richard Winter, *When Life Goes Dark: Finding Hope in the Midst of Depression* (Downers Grove, IL: InterVarsity Press, 2012); Amy Simpson, *Troubled Minds: Mental Illness and the Church's Mission* (Downers Grove, IL: InterVarsity Press, 2013); Ronald L. Koteskey, "What Missionaries Ought to Know about Depression," Missionary Care, www.mission arycare.com/brochures/br_depression.htm; YWAM Knowledge Base, "Depression," www.ywamkb.net/kb/Depression; and the *Christianity Today* March 2009 cover series: Dan G. Blazer, "The Depression Epidemic," www.christianitytoday.com/ct/2009/march/15.22.html; Mark R. McMinn, "When You're Depressed," www.christianitytoday.com/ct/2009/march/14.24.html; John Ortberg interview, "Connecting to Hope," www.christianitytoday.com/ct/2009/march/16.28.html.

[7]D. Martyn Lloyd-Jones, *Spiritual Depression: Its Causes and Cures* (Grand Rapids: Eerdmans, 1965), p. 19.

[8]See the following helpful books concerning spiritual warfare: Timothy Warner, *Spiritual Warfare: Victory over the Powers of This Dark World* (Wheaton, IL: Crossway Books, 1991); Thomas White, *The Believers Guide to Spiritual Warfare* (Ann Arbor, MI: Vine Books, 1990); Gregory Boyd, *God at War* (Downers Grove, IL: InterVarsity Press, 1997); Chuck Kraft and David Debord, *The Rules of Engagement* (Colorado Springs: Wagner Publications, 2000).

CHAPTER 11: SPIRITUAL KEY # 10: PURSUING A FOCUSED LIFE

[1]J. Robert Clinton, *Clinton's Biblical Leadership Commentary* (Altadena, CA: Barnabas Publishers, 1999), p. 403.

[2]Ibid., p. 407.

[3]Ibid., p. 515.

[4]Ibid , p. 514.

[5]Ibid., p. 516.

[6]Ibid., p. 514.

[7]J. Robert Clinton, *Titus: Apostolic Ministry* (Altadena, CA: Barnabas Publishers, 2001), p. 125.

[8]See Charles Hummel, *Tyranny of the Urgent* (Downers Grove, IL: Inter-Varsity Press, 1994).

Other Resources by Ryan Shaw

WAKING THE GIANT

College campuses and ministries around the world have historically been primary places where laborers for the nations have been fashioned by the hand of God. *Waking the Giant* envisions local churches, campus ministry fellowships and Bible schools to respond to the heart of God and to be set ablaze through a grassroots mobilization movement for the nations. An essential for influencers impacting their ministries for the nations.

ENGAGING THE HOLY SPIRIT

The Holy Spirit is the key to unlocking the potential of the body of Christ toward the fulfillment of the Great Commission. For many, he has become shrouded in misunderstanding, tension and debate. All disciples (no matter what theological affiliation) need a fuller, more balanced understanding of and engagement with the role and dynamics of the Spirit as he exalts Jesus in the Great Commission. He alone is the power behind the Great Commission.

CULTIVATING ABANDONED DEVOTION FOR JESUS SERIES

The Bible comes alive through these in-depth studies of Bible books and passages. With anointed insight and practical application, you will be propelled in cultivating a lifestyle of "abandoned devotion" to Jesus. The life of Joseph, book of Colossians, Jonah, Habakkuk and more. For use as an individual or group study. Your spiritual life will be fueled through these studies!

For more information about resources by Ryan Shaw and Student Volunteer Movement 2 (SVM2), visit www.SVM2.net or contact info@SVM2.net.

Student Volunteer Movement 2

WHAT IS STUDENT VOLUNTEER MOVEMENT 2 (SVM2)?

SVM2 is an informal, international alliance of individual local ministries (local churches, campus ministry fellowships, Bible schools/ Christian colleges) educating, inspiring and activating disciples for the fulfillment of the Great Commission. It's internationally structured around National Alliances made up of local ministries, called Great Commission Ministries, dedicated to implementing core tools for mobilization within their fellowships. National Alliances are being developed toward increasing mobilization movements to unreached and unengaged people groups. The shared corporate vision is the *fulfillment of the Great Commission in this generation.*

Over one hundred years ago, a generation from the United States, Canada and England took up God's invitation to work toward the fulfillment of the Great Commission. Today, the spirit of that movement continues, not primarily in the Western world but now across the global body of Christ as we together are activated toward the *fulfillment of the Great Commission in this generation.*

SVM2 is a mobilization initiative equipping local ministries to rightly engage in crosscultural mission through every believer playing his or her role in serving the Great Commission (going, giving, prayer/intercession, advocating for the unreached, mobilizing and more). SVM2's two-pronged approach is provoking spiritual awakening in the body of Christ, producing abandoned devotion to Jesus toward a global harvest among unreached and unengaged people groups.

HOW SVM2 SERVES

SVM2 serves the mobilization of the body of Christ toward the fulfillment of the Great Commission in many ways:

- *Four Core Components:* proven mobilization tools for Great Commission Ministries
- *IGNITE Media:* equipping articles, books, Bible studies and more to mobilize ministries
- *National Alliance Tours:* mobilizing and empowering ministries as Great Commission Ministries
- Conferences and consultations
- Abandoned Devotion gatherings
- 21 Days for Global Harvest annual prayer campaign
- Great Commission Equipping Center
- Global Harvest Prayer Room

IS YOUR LOCAL MINISTRY BECOMING A GREAT COMMISSION MINISTRY?

Visit us soon at SVM2.net!

GREAT COMMISSION EQUIPPING CENTER

SVM2's international office and equipping base is in beautiful Chiang Mai, Thailand, in the heart of Asia. Visit Chiang Mai and the Equipping Center, and participate in a variety of training programs serving the fulfillment of the Great Commission.

> *Mobilizer Equipping School.* This eight-week experience deepens the spiritual life of crosscultural mission mobilizers while equipping them with the foundations of the mission movement. Mobilizers are equipped to mobilize ministries in their home nations for crosscultural mission among the unreached.

Great Commission Institute. A three-week experience equipping ministry leaders with a deeper practical grasp of the Great Commission, cultivating deep spiritual life to appropriately advance it, its strategic themes, primary strategies, tools to mobilize their fellowships and specific roles every disciple plays in its fulfillment.

Spiritual Equipping for Message Bearers. A ten-day experience equipping current and prospective message bearers with essential spiritual keys to thrive in serving God. Teaching, dynamic reflection, hours in the Global Harvest Prayer Room and prayer counseling make for an impactful experience.

Global Harvest Prayer Room. The prayer room provides ongoing prayer and intercession mixed with worship toward the fulfillment of the Great Commission in this generation. Contending for spiritual awakening of the church and global harvest among the nations, Jesus is exalted over Thailand and the world.

Come be equipped in beautiful Chiang Mai! Visit the Equipping Center for a particular program or during a vacation, as part of a mission trip or to come and pray for awakening and harvest in the Global Harvest Prayer Room. Come for a few days, weeks or months.

Want to serve? Join the SVM2 team in Chiang Mai as regular or intercessory staff.

- *Regular staff* relocate to Chiang Mai for two to three years and participate in a variety of roles and activities supporting the international SVM2 initiative while spending seven to ten hours a week in the Global Harvest Prayer Room.

- *Intercessory staff* come to Chiang Mai for one- to three-month periods, spending twenty-one hours a week in the Global Harvest Prayer Room while participating in courses on prayer walks in the city and contributing to various SVM2 ministry projects.

JOIN THE CONVERSATION

- *Abandoned Times Blog:* free subscription at SVM2.net/aban donedtimes; twice-weekly posts on spiritual life, revival and crosscultural mission

- *Facebook:* www.facebook.com/pages/Student-Volunteer-Movement-2/60542404994

- *Twitter:* @SVM2

- *Web:* www.SVM2.net